THE LION'S HONEY

Grace for flawed Christian leaders

John Benton

EP BOOKS
1st Floor Venture House, 6 Silver Court, Watchmead,
Welwyn Garden City, UK, AL7 1TS

web: http://www.epbooks.org

e-mail: sales@epbooks.org

EP Books are distributed in the USA by:
JPL Distribution
3741 Linden Avenue Southeast
Grand Rapids, MI 49548
E-mail: orders@jplbooks.com
Tel: 877.683.6935

© John Benton 2016. All rights reserved. No part of this publication may be reproduced, stored in a retrieval system or transmitted, in any form, or by any means, electronic, mechanical, photocopying, recording or otherwise, without the prior permission of the publishers.

British Library Cataloguing in Publication Data available

ISBN 978–1–78397–181–7

Unless otherwise indicated, Scripture quotations in this publication are from the THE HOLY BIBLE, NEW INTERNATIONAL VERSION® NIV® Copyright © 1973, 1978, 1984 by International Bible Society® Used by permission. All rights reserved worldwide.

I am very much indebted to my dear friend Rosemary Smith for all her help with the manuscript and also for the great encouragement she has given me to get this material on Samson published.

Contents

Introduction	7
1. The lens of idolatry	11
2. What is idolatry?	15
3. Samson's story	21
4. Portrait of a hero	33
5. Uncovering Samson's idols	49
6. What a man like Samson needs to hear	63
7. A profound repentance, an outrageous faith	91
Notes	99

Introduction

God doesn't always choose regular men as leaders. Sometimes he opts for characters who are flawed, unusual and not those that the church would automatically light upon. It is as if the Lord takes a risk.

The pathway to the ministry has become quite standardized in recent years in the UK. When we look at the typical CV of candidates for leading a church, we are usually looking at young men from middle-class Christian homes who have been to university and perhaps spent some time in student work or in a respectable profession having, at some point, sailed through an accredited evangelical Bible college. There they are, scrubbed up nicely, raring to go and full of ideas. And there's nothing wrong with that.

Amazing grace

But some men upon whom God lays his hand are different. They don't come from a Christian family. Or if they do, it wasn't a good one. They may not have been to college. They may have had a life on the streets. And before they were converted their way was one of which they are now ashamed and which has left them with ongoing struggles. Yet God has called them into ministry.

It does happen. Augustine of Hippo had a past life worthy of shocked tabloid headlines in any century and a Christian mother who, it seems, had a drink problem. John Newton wrote the much-loved gospel song *Amazing Grace* exactly because he was truly amazed that God should save and call into Christian service someone like himself with a wayward past and a background full of blasphemy and cursing in the awful trade of slavery and human trafficking. Yet, despite their scarlet sins, God claimed them and used them for his purposes.

Damaged goods

Our own sins always leave scars on us. These can go deep. There are also the bruises that come from being on the wrong end of other peoples' sins. No one has a perfect past or a perfect upbringing. So Christian leaders can be damaged goods. Furthermore, each of us, no matter how 'regular' we may appear outwardly, has his own weaknesses. And for some there are psychologically subterranean issues with which we struggle. Yes, thank God, we meet the requirements of character and behaviour set out in the New Testament for leaders in 1 Timothy 3 and Titus 1. But some of us may have to work much harder than others to make the grade.

We have a wild side lurking within us, which can be dangerous to God's church. Though it is perhaps hidden under a disguise of public godliness, untamed sin and the idols of the heart that lead to self-pity, over-bearing pride, perverse sexual temptations and other defective personality traits lie just beneath the surface. On his worst days, a Christian leader might actually be frightened of himself and what he is capable of, apart from God's grace. Here we are called to be a blessing to the church but we could so easily be the opposite.

How are we to deal with that? If you are such a Christian leader, what are you to do? We are people who love God but who know we are dangerously blemished.

Samson

Such thoughts lead us to think about the Old Testament hero Samson. It would be an understatement to call him 'unusual'. His life seems constantly stained by revenge and terrible moral failure. As we meet him in Scripture and consider his life we soon recognize him not only as a very powerful but also a very complex character. He was a remarkably gifted man but just as capable of bringing trouble on God's people as blessing (Judges 15:9–12). Physically and mentally strong, yet he was morally weak.

If you feel your weaknesses as a church leader, this book is for you. If you are aware you have serious issues that need addressing, keep reading.

Early on in my Christian life I recognized something of my own inner problems. And then God called me to be a preacher and a pastor! I was overjoyed but simultaneously worried. Could I be the man God had called me to be? It felt pretty uncomfortable.

But a few years into my ministry, an assignment to study the life of Samson led to some vital discoveries. What I found made me much more aware of myself and of the particular areas where I needed the grace of God. Understanding this unusual and obviously defective man Samson has played no small part in keeping me in the ministry and, hopefully, not doing too much damage.

It is my hope that this short study of the life of Samson as a defective Christian leader will enable others to be honest, and to understand themselves and to persevere in fruitful ministry. We are going to start by thinking about how best to diagnose the flaws deep within our hearts.

1. The lens of idolatry

A vet is in his surgery looking at a cat that seems to be lying calmly on the operating table. He deploys his stethoscope. He hears nothing. He shakes the stethoscope thinking it may be malfunctioning and tries again. Still nothing. The animal is showing no heartbeat. He panics. 'Karen', he shouts to his assistant, 'I've got a cat here with no pulse! I need adrenalin and an IV line as soon as possible!' She rushes in only to slow down and then smile knowingly as she recovers her fur hat from under the vet's deficient gaze.

It's an advert. He needs spectacles.

Sometimes we require a new pair of glasses in order to see the things we need to see. The Bible has a lot to say on the subject of idolatry and to think in terms of idolatry actually provides us with a marvellously effective biblical lens through which to see and understand our sin. This is especially true when it comes to diagnosing what some people call 'the sin under the sin'. It exposes our undercover self-deceptions.

The fall of leaders

This is a book about preventing ministerial failure. It is about how, despite our flaws, to avoid being a church leader who falls by the wayside. Sadly, ministerial failure is a phenomenon that is all too common in the twenty-first century. Good men, gifted men, zealous and sincere men take on church leadership. There are many excellent Bible colleges and training courses that seek to equip and propel their students into the task of pastoring and growing churches through the preaching of God's word. But statistics show that the subsequent dropout rate is quite alarming. Many stumble and fall. This may be through 'burn out'—overwork and prolonged disappointment. It may be through catastrophic sin. Leaders have to leave their posts. Often all this is very damaging to the church.

I listened recently to the principal of a well-known evangelical college in the UK who spoke of a ten-year watershed. If they last 10 years, men are likely to stick at the ministry right through their working lives. But many of his students, he found, were not lasting a decade. Quite a few were leaving the ministry long before that.

Roots in the heart

But ministerial failure does not come out of the blue. Be it through exhaustion, gradual decline or a sudden moral disaster, it does not happen by chance. It is not simply an inexplicable tragedy. It always has its roots in the heart. It is to do with 'the sin beneath the sin'.

How do we get to see what's going on in the heart? It is

here that we need to deploy the biblical lens of idolatry to investigate ourselves and look beneath the surface of our lives.

Human failings can be likened to an iceberg. Only one tenth is seen above the surface. Nine tenths lies hidden under the ocean. The sins and failures that break surface in our lives are the product of what goes on in the secret subterranean depths of our hearts—what we desire, what we tell ourselves inwardly. Jesus pointed to this when he explained that 'evils come from inside' (Mark 7:23). Jeremiah taught the same when he wrote, 'The heart is deceitful above all things and beyond cure; who can understand it?' (Jeremiah 17:9). The writer of Proverbs tells us that 'The purposes of a man's heart are deep waters' and not everyone can discern what is there (Proverbs 20:5).

The investigative lens of asking ourselves about idolatry in our lives gives us a way of seeing inside ourselves. It enables us to plumb the depths of our hearts. It provides us with an endoscopy of our inner being.

Hidden idols

We are going to look at a case study of Samson. He was, as we shall see, a man with hidden depths and hidden idols. We find his story in the Old Testament book of Judges. He was one of God's leaders who made a huge mess of things. We are going to look at what the Bible records about this man and try to uncover the idols of his heart, which led him astray, caused him so much pain and eventually destroyed him (though not without accomplishing something for God). As we do this, hopefully we will get insight into our own hearts and our own idols. We will understand what goes on inside us. We will question ourselves. We will understand ourselves in a more realistic way and so see the continuing need we have for God's mercy and grace as his children.

Samson 'messed up big time' as we say. But he made mistakes from which we can learn. He really crashed and burned. Yet, praise God, we find there was grace for him and ultimate victory. Although this book is about someone who went disastrously astray, it is also a book of hope. We live under the new covenant introduced by the Lord Jesus Christ and we shall find that there is an astounding sufficiency in Christ to meet our deepest needs and keep us in his service no matter how 'unusual' or flawed we may feel ourselves to be.

2. What is idolatry?

When we think of idolatry, the classic example that comes to mind is that of Israel making and worshipping the golden calf. It is an incident that astonishes us. Though the living God had just rescued the nation from the slave camps of Pharaoh's Egypt through the apocalyptic plagues and the parting of the Red Sea, yet when Moses, their leader, left them to spend time with God on Mount Sinai, they quickly made a 'god' of their own.

And, shamefully, we are just the same.

Being twenty-first century people we may dismiss worshipping idols as belonging to what we see as the ignorance of ancient history. But, of course, we must not restrict the idea of idolatry to bowing down to figures of metal, wood or stone. Idolatry is really a matter of the inner life. That is why, if we can identify our idols, we find out so much about ourselves.

Where is your heart?

Idolatry is about the heart. A recurring theme in the histories of the Old Testament kings is their propensity to become idolaters. It always led to trouble. For example, concerning the final chapter of Solomon's life we are told 'his wives turned his heart after other gods ...' 1 Kings 11:4. Notice from his *heart* Solomon embraced the foreign idols. Soon afterwards the holy nation barely avoided civil war and split into two with great bitterness on both sides. Scripture traces this all back to what went on in Solomon's heart. And as soon as the division of the nation was complete, the new northern nation of Israel set up idols—basically two golden calves at Bethel and Dan (1 Kings 12:25–30), reminiscent of the Exodus incident. They took the road their wayward forefathers had taken. Founded on idolatry, Israel was later destroyed by the Assyrians.

Judah remained. But, moving on in Bible history, the prophetess Huldah explained the reason for the subsequent destruction of Jerusalem, Judah's capital city, by the Babylonians, and the exile of its people. Through her the LORD says, 'Because they have forsaken me and burned incense to other gods and provoked me to anger by all that their hands have made, my anger will be poured out on this place and will not be quenched' (2 Chronicles 34:25). An idolatrous heart does real damage to God's people and his work.

The New Testament recognizes the same truth. Idolatry is not simply an outward act of genuflecting before some material object but an inward commitment and attraction.

Paul speaks in Colossians 3:5, for example, of 'evil desires and greed which is idolatry'.

And when it comes to the inner life, Christians can be just as prone to idolatry as anyone else. That is why the apostle John's punch-line, probably summarizing the thrust of his first epistle, is 'Dear children, keep yourselves from idols' (1 John 5:21).

A definition

What is an idol? We can put it like this: An idol is anything we pursue apart from God, which we believe will satisfy us in a way God cannot or will not.[1]

It is anything that we put in the place that should be reserved for God alone. It is whatever we place our hopes in for joy and life.

Martin Luther, in his Larger Catechism discussion of the first of the ten commandments says this: 'Whatever your heart clings to and relies upon, that is your God; trust and faith of the heart alone make both God and idol.'[2]

Who or what is really your God? We are going to be asking that question of Samson and by implication of ourselves. It is whatever you rely on for your happiness and ultimate security.

What's the attraction?

Why are we attracted to idols? It goes back to our fallen, sinful, unbelieving nature. It is because idols hold out a deceptive promise. It is because they are very different from the living God. They appear to have power and to be under *our* control, whereas no one controls or can control the LORD.

The idea of power and happiness placed in our hands, that it is possible for us to manipulate, to use as we would like, appeals to us. Hence money and wealth are such popular gods. They give us power to get what we think will make us happy. As egotistical sinners, we want to be masters not servants. We can spend our money on whatever we want. Money puts us in the driving seat. And we want to be at the steering wheel. Idols are just another avenue of appearing to fulfil the promise the snake made in the garden of Eden to Adam and Eve, 'You will be like God' (Genesis 3:5).

But idols have a propensity to ensnare us and destroy us.

The old 1969 film, *The Italian Job*, always reminds us of this fact. The movie stars Michael Caine (Charlie Croker) and Noel Coward (Mr Bridger) and has become a classic. Backed by Mr Bridger, the head of a large criminal syndicate that he operates from prison, cockney gangster Charlie Croker assembles a team to steal $4 million in gold (a great deal of money in 1969) from a place in Italy using three Austin minis—iconic British cars of the 1960s. The plot proceeds with humour along the way. The gang manages the theft, with exciting car chases through an enormous city-wide traffic jam, and transfer the gold onto an innocent-looking coach before seeking to get away over the Alps into Switzerland.

But the film ends on a cliff-hanger—literally. On the mountain roads, the coach skids and its back end is left teetering over a precipice with the gold bullion having slid towards the rear doors. Only the body weight of the thieves at the other end of the vehicle maintains the balance which avoids disaster. As Croker attempts to get to the gold, the equilibrium is disturbed and the gold slips further away. The whole vehicle, villains included, could easily topple over the edge to destruction.

Gold, and the wealth and power it epitomizes, is the idol. But if the team try to go and take possession of it, it will take them over the cliff to their deaths. They could simply get off the coach and save their lives, but that would mean the coach and the gold going over the edge and being lost. They feel they can't let it go. It's so valuable. It means too much to them. They are trapped in the coach by their desire for the gold. The film ends with Charlie announcing that he has a 'great idea.' Those words signal his enslavement. He can't let the gold go. The idol has them in its power.

That is how it is with idols—whether it's money, power, sex, a demon god, or something else. Though they hold out the promise of security and happiness, they will seek to trap us and destroy us.

Idols of the heart are a real threat to churches and to Christian leaders.

3. Samson's story

We are going to use the biblical biography of Samson found in Judges chapters 13 to 16 as a case study of a Christian leader destroyed by deep idols.

But first, if we are going to do that, we had better familiarize ourselves with Samson's story. Don't skip this. Let's read through the text of Judges 13–16.

The Birth of Samson

13 *Again the Israelites did evil in the eyes of the Lord, so the* Lord *delivered them into the hands of the Philistines for forty years.*

² A certain man of Zorah, named Manoah, from the clan of the Danites, had a wife who was sterile, and remained childless. ³ The angel of the Lord *appeared to her and said, 'You are sterile and childless, but you are going to conceive and have a son. ⁴ Now see to it that you drink no wine or other fermented drink and that you do not eat anything unclean. ⁵ because you will conceive and have a son. No razor may be used on his head because the boy is to be a Nazirite,* set apart to God from birth and he will begin the deliverance of Israel from the hands of the Philistines.'

6 Then the woman went to her husband and told him, 'A man of God came to me. He looked like an angel of God, very awesome. I didn't ask him where he came from, and he didn't tell me his name. 7 But he said to me, "You will conceive and give birth to a son. Now then, drink no wine or other fermented drink and do not eat anything unclean, because the boy will be a Nazirite of God from birth until the day of his death."'

8 Then Manoah prayed to the LORD: 'O Lord, I beg you, let the man of God you sent to us come again to teach us how to bring up the boy who is to be born.'

9 God heard Manoah, and the angel of God came again to the woman while she was out in the field; but her husband Manoah was not with her. 10 The woman hurried to tell her husband, 'He's here! The man who appeared to me the other day!'

11 Manoah got up and followed his wife. When he came to the man, he said, 'Are you the one who talked to my wife?'

'I am,' he said.

12 So Manoah asked him, 'When your words are fulfilled, what is to be the rule for the boy's life and work?'

13 The angel of the LORD answered, 'Your wife must do all that I have told her. 14 She must not eat anything that comes from the grapevine, nor drink any wine or other fermented drink nor eat anything unclean. She must do everything I have commanded her.'

15 Manoah said to the angel of the LORD, 'We would like you to stay until we prepare a young goat for you.'

16 *The angel of the* Lord *replied, 'Even though you detain me, I will not eat any of your food. But if you prepare a burnt offering, offer it to the* Lord*.' (Manoah did not realize that it was the angel of the* Lord*).*

17 *Then Manoah inquired of the angel of the* Lord*, 'What is your name, so that we may honour you when your word comes true?'*

18 *He replied, 'Why do you ask my name? It is beyond understanding.'* 19 *Then Manoah took a young goat, together with the grain offering, and sacrificed it on a rock to the* Lord*. And the* Lord *did an amazing thing while Manoah and his wife watched:* 20 *As the flame blazed up from the altar toward heaven, the angel of the* Lord *ascended in the flame. Seeing this, Manoah and his wife fell with their faces to the ground.* 21 *When the angel of the* Lord *did not show himself again to Manoah and his wife, Manoah realized that it was the angel of the* Lord*.*

22 *'We are doomed to die!' he said to his wife. 'We have seen God!'*

23 *But his wife answered, 'If the* Lord *had meant to kill us, he would not have accepted a burnt offering and grain offering from our hands, nor shown us all these things or now told us this.'*

24 *The woman gave birth to a boy and named him Samson. He grew and the* Lord *blessed him,* 25 *and the Spirit of the* Lord *began to stir him while he was in Mahaneh Dan, between Zorah and Eshtaol.*

Samson's Marriage

14 *Samson went down to Timnah and saw there a young Philistine woman.* 2 *When he returned, he said to his father and mother, 'I have seen a Philistine woman in Timnah; now get her for me as my wife.'*

3 *His father and mother replied, 'Isn't there an acceptable woman*

among your relatives or among all our people? Must you go to the uncircumcised Philistines to get a wife?'

But Samson said to his father, 'Get her for me. She's the right one for me.' 4 (His parents did not know that this was from the LORD, who was seeking an occasion to confront the Philistines; for at that time they were ruling over Israel.)

5 Samson went down to Timnah together with his father and mother. As they approached the vineyards of Timnah, suddenly a young lion came roaring toward him. 6 The Spirit of the LORD came upon him in power so that he tore the lion apart with his bare hands as he might have torn a young goat. But he told neither his father nor his mother what he had done. 7 Then he went down and talked with the woman, and he liked her.

8 Some time later, when he went back to marry her, he turned aside to look at the lion's carcass. In it he saw a swarm of bees and some honey. 9 which he scooped out with his hands and ate as he went along. When he rejoined his parents, he gave them some, and they too ate it. But he did not tell them that he had taken the honey from the lion's carcass.

10 Now his father went down to see the woman. And Samson held a feast there, as was customary for bridegrooms. 11 When he appeared, he was given thirty companions.

12 'Let me tell you a riddle,' Samson said to them. 'If you can give me the answer within the seven days of the feast, I will give you thirty linen garments and thirty sets of clothes. 13 If you can't tell me the answer, you must give me thirty linen garments and thirty sets of clothes.'

'Tell us your riddle,' they said. 'Let's hear it.'

¹⁴ He replied,

'Out of the eater, something to eat;
out of the strong, something sweet.'
For three days they could not give the answer.

¹⁵ On the fourth day, they said to Samson's wife, 'Coax your husband into explaining the riddle for us, or we will burn you and your father's household to death. Did you invite us here to rob us?'

¹⁶ Then Samson's wife threw herself on him, sobbing, 'You hate me! You don't really love me. You've given my people a riddle, but you haven't told me the answer.'

'I haven't even explained it to my father or mother,' he replied, 'so why should I explain it to you?' ¹⁷ She cried the whole seven days of the feast. So on the seventh day he finally told her, because she continued to press him. She in turn explained the riddle to her people.

¹⁸ Before sunset on the seventh day the men of the town said to him,

'What is sweeter than honey?
What is stronger than a lion?'

Samson said to them,

'If you had not ploughed with my heifer,
you would not have solved my riddle.'

¹⁹ Then the Spirit of the LORD came upon him in power. He went down to Ashkelon, struck down thirty of their men, stripped them of their belongings and gave their clothes to those who had explained the riddle. Burning with anger, he went up to his father's house. ²⁰ And Samson's wife was given to the friend who had attended him at his wedding.

Samson's Vengeance on the Philistines

15 *Later on, at the time of wheat harvest, Samson took a young goat and went to visit his wife. He said, 'I'm going to my wife's room.' But her father would not let him go in.*

² *'I was so sure you thoroughly hated her,' he said, 'that I gave her to your friend. Isn't her younger sister more attractive? Take her instead.'*

³ *Samson said to them, 'This time I have a right to get even with the Philistines; I will really harm them.'* ⁴ *So he went out and caught three hundred foxes and tied them tail to tail in pairs. He then fastened a torch to every pair of tails,* ⁵ *lit the torches and let the foxes loose in the standing corn of the Philistines. He burned up the shocks and standing corn, together with the vineyards and olive groves.*

⁶ *When the Philistines asked, 'Who did this?' they were told, 'Samson, the Timnite's son-in-law, because his wife was given to his friend.'*

So the Philistines went up and burned her and her father to death. ⁷ *Samson said to them, 'Since you've acted like this, I won't stop until I get my revenge on you.'* ⁸ *He attacked them viciously and slaughtered many of them. Then he went down and stayed in a cave in the rock of Etam.*

⁹ *The Philistines went up and camped in Judah, spreading out near Lehi.* ¹⁰ *The men of Judah asked, 'Why have you come to fight us?'*

'We have come to take Samson prisoner,' they answered, 'to do to him as he did to us.'

¹¹ *Then three thousand men from Judah went down to the cave in the rock of Etam and said to Samson, 'Don't you realize that the Philistines are rulers over us? What have you done to us?'*

He answered, 'I merely did to them what they did to me.'

¹² They said to him, 'We've come to tie you up and hand you over to the Philistines.'

Samson said, 'Swear to me that you won't kill me yourselves.'

¹³ 'Agreed,' they answered. 'We will only tie you up and hand you over to them. We will not kill you.' So they bound him with two new ropes and led him up from the rock. ¹⁴ As he approached Lehi, the Philistines came toward him shouting. The Spirit of the LORD came upon him in power. The ropes on his arms became like charred flax, and the bindings dropped from his hands. ¹⁵ Finding a fresh jawbone of a donkey, he grabbed it and struck down a thousand men.

¹⁶ Then Samson said,

'With a donkey's jaw-bone
I have made donkeys of them.
With a donkey's jaw-bone
I have killed a thousand men.'

¹⁷ When he finished speaking, he threw away the jawbone; and the place was called Ramath Lehi.

¹⁸ Because he was very thirsty, he cried out to the LORD, 'You have given your servant this great victory. Must I now die of thirst and fall into the hands of the uncircumcised?' ¹⁹ Then God opened up the hollow place in Lehi, and water came out of it. When Samson drank, his strength returned and he revived. So the spring was called En Hakkore, and it is still there in Lehi.

²⁰ Samson led Israel for twenty years in the days of the Philistines.

Samson and Delilah

16 One day Samson went to Gaza, where he saw a prostitute. He went in to spend the night with her. ² The people of Gaza were told, 'Samson is here!' So they surrounded the place and lay in wait for him all night at the city gate. They made no move during the night, saying, 'At dawn we'll kill him.'

3 But Samson lay there only until the middle of the night. Then he got up and took hold of the doors of the city gate, together with the two posts, and tore them loose, bar and all. He lifted them to his shoulders and carried them to the top of the hill that faces Hebron.

4 Some time later, he fell in love with a woman in the Valley of Sorek whose name was Delilah. 5 The rulers of the Philistines went to her and said, 'See if you can lure him into showing you the secret of his great strength and how we can overpower him so we may tie him up and subdue him. Each one of us will give you eleven hundred shekels of silver.'

6 So Delilah said to Samson, 'Tell me the secret of your great strength and how you can be tied up and subdued.'

7 Samson answered her, 'If anyone ties me with seven fresh thongs that have not been dried, I'll become as weak as any other man.'

8 Then the rulers of the Philistines brought her seven fresh thongs that had not been dried, and she tied him with them. 9 With men hidden in the room, she called to him, 'Samson, the Philistines are upon you!' But he snapped the thongs as easily as a piece of string snaps when it comes close to a flame. So the secret of his strength was not discovered.

10 Then Delilah said to Samson, 'You have made a fool of me; you lied to me. Come now, tell me how you can be tied.'

11 He said, 'If anyone ties me securely with new ropes that have never been used, I'll become as weak as any other man.'

12 So Delilah took new ropes and tied him with them. Then, with

men hidden in the room, she called to him, 'Samson, the Philistines are upon you!' But he snapped the ropes off his arms as if they were threads.

13 Delilah then said to Samson, 'Until now, you have been making a fool of me and lying to me. Tell me how you can be tied.'

He replied, 'If you weave the seven braids of my head into the fabric on the loom and tighten it with the pin, I'll become as weak as any other man.' So while he was sleeping, Delilah took the seven braids of his head, wove them into the fabric 14 and tightened it with the pin.

Again she called to him, 'Samson, the Philistines are upon you!' He awoke from his sleep and pulled up the pin and the loom, with the fabric.

15 Then she said to him, 'How can you say, "I love you," when you won't confide in me? This is the third time you have made a fool of me and haven't told me the secret of your great strength.' 16 With such nagging she prodded him day after day until he was tired to death.

17 So he told her everything. 'No razor has ever been used on my head,' he said, 'because I have been a Nazirite set apart to God since birth. If my head were shaved, my strength would leave me, and I would become as weak as any other man.'

18 When Delilah saw that he had told her everything, she sent word to the rulers of the Philistines, 'Come back once more; he has told me everything.' So the rulers of the Philistines returned with the silver in their hands. 19 Having put him to sleep on her lap, she called a man to shave off the seven braids of his hair, and so began to subdue him. And his strength left him.

20 Then she called, 'Samson, the Philistines are upon you!'

He awoke from his sleep and thought, 'I'll go out as before and shake myself free.' But he did not know that the LORD had left him.

21 *Then the Philistines seized him, gouged out his eyes and took him down to Gaza. Binding him with bronze shackles, they set him to grinding in the prison.* 22 *But the hair on his head began to grow again after it had been shaved.*

The Death of Samson

23 *Now the rulers of the Philistines assembled to offer a great sacrifice to Dagon their god and to celebrate, saying, 'Our god has delivered Samson, our enemy, into our hands.'*

24 *When the people saw him, they praised their god, saying,*

*'Our god has delivered our enemy
into our hands,
the one who laid waste our land
and multiplied our slain.'*

25 *While they were in high spirits, they shouted, 'Bring out Samson to entertain us.' So they called Samson out of the prison, and he performed for them.*

When they stood him among the pillars, 26 *Samson said to the servant who held his hand, 'Put me where I can feel the pillars that support the temple, so that I may lean against them.'* 27 *Now the temple was crowded with men and women; all the rulers of the Philistines were there, and on the roof were about three thousand men and women watching Samson perform.* 28 *Then Samson prayed to the LORD, 'O Sovereign LORD, remember me. O God, please strengthen me just once more, and let me with one blow get revenge on the Philistines for my two eyes.'* 29 *Then Samson reached toward the two central pillars on which the temple stood. Bracing himself against them, his right hand on the one and his left hand on the other,* ³⁰ *Samson said, 'Let me die with the Philistines!' Then he pushed with all his might, and down came the temple on the rulers and all the people in it. Thus he killed many more when he died than while he lived.*

³¹ *Then his brothers and his father's whole family went down to get him. They brought him back and buried him between Zorah and Eshtaol in the tomb of Manoah his father. He had led Israel twenty years.*

What a story! It might be good, having read through Samson's life, just to think about it for yourself for a moment.

Chronologically, the story unfolds in five sections: Samson's birth, Samson's marriage, Samson's vengeance, Samson's seduction and Samson's death.

But ask yourself some questions and make some notes. How would you describe Samson as a man? What do you think were the driving motivations in his life? How would you describe his relationship with God? Why do you think he was so vulnerable to sensual pleasures? What was his chief goal in life? How do you think you might be like Samson?

We are going to be looking at questions like these as our study progresses, but it would be good if you thought about these things for yourself first in order to really engage with our subject before we proceed.

4. Portrait of a hero

Having read the story and tried to get our minds in gear with respect to Samson, let's attempt to organize the data concerning him not so much according to chronology, or even theology, but according to 'psychology'. We will seek to piece together a picture of the man, the pressures on him and his behaviour. We do this in order that we can discover what is driving him and so understand his heart and the idols residing there.

God's child

As we embark on this journey, the first thing to be clear on is that this man Samson was a child of God. The way he behaves at times you can hardly believe it. But he is listed among the heroes of faith in the great gallery of God's servants in chapter 11 of the New Testament book of Hebrews.

Having commended Abel and Enoch and Noah and Abraham and Moses and Rahab, the writer continues,

'And what more shall I say? I do not have time to tell about Gideon, Barak, Samson, Jephthah, David and Samuel and the prophets, who through faith conquered kingdoms, administered justice, and gained what was promised; who shut the mouths of lions, quenched the fury of the flames, and escaped the edge of the sword; whose weakness was turned to strength, and who became powerful in battle, and routed foreign armies' (Hebrews 11:32, 33). There is our man in verse 32, set right alongside David and Samuel no less. He is a man God uses. He belongs to the Lord. And in his sovereignty, God even utilizes Samson's ungodly attitudes on occasions.

Under God, he achieves much against the enemies of God's people.

But, although he is a child of God, Samson is a child of God who comes with a health warning for us. Yes, he was a man of faith and we must follow him in that. But, by and large, we are to learn from Samson's mistakes not his example. If Othniel (Judges 3:7–11) is the first judge who provides a template for others to follow, then by the time of Samson, that template is very much defaced.

Character study?

At this point someone may raise a question. Are we meant to study Samson's life in this way?

The primary theological purpose of the book of Judges is not to provide us with character studies. It is, of course, to point us to our God, the great Saviour of rebel sinners like ourselves. Judges shows that the Lord is never at a loss to find the means to save sinners who cry to him. It builds our faith. If God can save through a wayward man like Samson, how much more can he save us through his perfect Son, the Lord Jesus Christ.

With all his sinful behaviour, we may wonder why Judges gives so much space to Samson—four whole chapters out of twenty-one. That's almost a fifth of the book. Why does he get so much exposure?

Edmund Clowney, in his short and fascinating Biblical theology of the Old Testament, *The Unfolding Mystery*, sets us in the right direction to answer that question. Under the female judge Deborah, and under Gideon and then Jephthah, the people of Israel were up for a fight. They were oppressed by their enemies but nevertheless, at the call of the judge, they were prepared to take up their weapons and fight for their freedom (Judges 4:10; 6:34, 35; 11:11).

But by the time we get to Samson, it seems that all the fight had gone out of Israel. He is rejected by Israel. The men of Judah would rather hand Samson over to the Philistines to save their skins than follow him into battle (Judges 15:12). Samson stood alone.

But God's Spirit came upon God's servant Samson, and, with the super-human strength infused into this man, God showed he was able to deliver his people using just a single man. Referring back to Gideon's story, Edmund Clowney writes: 'When the Spirit of God came upon Samson, the Lord showed that He had no need even for three hundred. He could deliver by one.'[1]

Thus Samson becomes a magnificent type of the Lord Jesus

Christ, God's great servant and Saviour, rejected by men, but who single-handedly has dealt the death blow to our terrible enemies of sin, hell and Satan. We are reminded of Paul's words in Romans 5:19 as he compares and contrasts Adam and Christ: 'For just as through the disobedience of the one man the many were made sinners, so also through the obedience of the one man the many will be made righteous.' Solitary Samson points gloriously to Jesus.

But having recognized that Judges is first of all Christological, as is all the Old Testament, nevertheless we are meant to draw lessons for our lives from the characters we meet there. The New Testament is very clear that we are to learn lessons from the lives of those who have gone before us. For example, Paul tells us to take warning from the idolatry of Israel (1 Corinthians 10:6–13). Jude tells us to do the same (Jude v5–7). James clearly wants us to imitate the patience of Job and the believing prayer of Elijah (James 5:10, 11, 17, 18). Indeed Paul tells us that, 'Everything that was written in the past was written to teach us, so that through endurance and the encouragement of the Scriptures we might have hope' (Romans 15:4). So our character study approach is not without Scriptural foundation.

Birth and background

Let us now assemble a simple portrait of Samson's life, highlighting the main points. Church leader, perhaps you will find a few echoes of your own life here?

Samson was miraculously born.

Two things are worth underlining here. First, the

circumstances of Samson's birth to a previously barren woman (Judges 13:2,3) means, of course, that he was the first child in the family. Later other brothers were born (Judges 16:31) but Samson was the eldest son. Sometimes parents can both over-indulge a firstborn child. That might be especially true of parents who previously thought they would never have children. Are you a first-born child?

Second, along with his miraculous birth, the angel announcing his conception declared him to be a child of destiny, set apart to God from birth, who would one day begin to deliver Israel from the oppression of the Philistines. This would surely mean that Samson's parents had high expectations for him. How would Samson have reacted to that as he was growing up? Ask yourself.

On both these counts, Samson could have been looked upon with unusual favour and perhaps even spoiled by his inexperienced parents.

Samson was set apart to be a Nazirite.

The angel tells Samson's mother, 'You are sterile and childless, but you are going to conceive and have a son. Now see to it that you drink no wine or other fermented drink and that you do not eat anything unclean. because you will conceive and have a son. No razor may be used on his head, because the boy is to be a Nazirite to God from birth, and he will begin to save Israel from the hand of the Philistines' (Judges 13:3–5).

Not only is Samson recognized as a special child by his parents, he is also going to be a child separated to God. And he is going to be seen as different by his peers because of the requirements, including things like uncut hair, the Lord lays upon him as a Nazirite. He is going to stand out in a crowd.

The vow of the Nazirite is explained in Numbers 6. It was a way by which ordinary Israelite 'lay' people could express deep commitment to the Lord. This was symbolized in three areas: alcohol consumption, hair control and corpse contact.[2] Let's unpack this briefly.

First, let's look at alcohol consumption. Alcohol cheers the heart. By avoiding alcohol or any product of the vine it was a way of saying 'All my joy is found in the Lord' (cf. Psalm 104:15). It was a statement of glorying in God alone.

Second, there's hair control. Our hair grows because we are alive. It just happens. We don't have to do anything; it simply gets longer. Normally we have a haircut periodically. We bring that innate expression of life under our control. We impose order on it. But by not cutting his hair, the Nazirite was symbolizing the idea that his life was in God's control not his own. It was probably an expression of surrender to God.

Third, there is corpse contact. It was to be completely avoided. Biblically, death has come into the world through sin (Genesis 2:17; 3:19). Dead bodies were therefore a serious source of ritual uncleanness, barring people from the presence of the holy God of life. Therefore, by avoiding all contact with corpses, even those of near relatives, the Nazirite was seeking to be clean in God's sight and so know the Lord's nearness.

Thus, the Nazirite vow was a public declaration of

commitment to the Lord. As we read the regulations, we find the vow of the Nazirite was voluntary and usually a temporary vow (Numbers 6:5, 13).

But for Samson, this was to be a life-long dedication required by God. This need for life-long commitment probably reflected the dire situation in which the Israelite nation found itself during Samson's time. They were oppressed by mighty foes. They needed a rescuer totally dedicated to the Lord.

But that means that there was a lot of responsibility placed on Samson's shoulders. How would he handle that? Similarly, much responsibility rests upon the shoulders of church leaders. How do we react to that? Again, ask yourself.

Samson's relationship to his parents

Samson's mother seems a more mature character than his father. This might be partly why the Lord deals with her rather than her husband in sending the angel to her (13:3). Though of course it is she, as the woman who is going to be most directly involved with the birth of the child, it may be a sign of her greater spirituality too. Also, it is the father, Manoah, who is doubtful and anxious about the message his wife says she has received from the angel and he prays for the angel to return (13:8). And again, after the second visit of the angel of the Lord, it is Manoah who over-reacts and panicking, concludes: 'We are doomed to die, for we have seen God' (13:22), whereas his wife gives the sensible reasoning that if God intended to strike them down he would not have accepted their offering or foretold the birth of their child (13:23).

It would seem, therefore, that Manoah was a rather emotional, anxious individual who would be unlikely to provide a firm lead in the family and that his mother would have been the most weighty and best influence upon Samson. Indeed, it is she who is recorded as giving the child his name (13:24), an act most usually carried out by the father (cf. Genesis 21:3; Luke 1:63).

So, the impression given by the text is that, although they had their weaknesses, Samson had a loving regard for his parents, including them in his life.

However, two incidents stand out of which we should take note. First, when he says he wants to marry a Philistine girl rather than an Israelite woman, he simply brushes aside his parents' objections in an imperious, almost threatening, way (14:3). Yes, in God's sovereignty, this was 'from the LORD' as he planned under his providence to use Samson against the Philistines. But Samson's way of speaking to his parents seems disrespectful: 'Get her for me!' (14:4).

Second, it would seem from the incident of killing the lion, that Samson kept secret from his parents some of his activities. 'He told neither his father nor his mother what he had done' (14:6). A man doesn't have to share everything with his close relatives. But having accomplished such a feat, it would be natural to think he would want to tell his parents. But he doesn't. Samson operates covertly, independently.

This matrix of behaviour would fit with our picture of Manoah as a less-than-firm father who would probably have felt unable to discipline his powerful growing eldest son, who was to be God's chosen deliverer.

The Bible recognizes that our upbringing by our parents has a marked effect upon us as people (Proverbs 1:8,9; Proverbs 3:11,12; Proverbs 13:1 etc.). We are not to let the lack of a perfect upbringing become an excuse for bad ways, but it can be helpful in understanding ourselves to reflect on our childhood experiences and how they might have shaped our choices and what we might have set our hearts on in life. In other words, sometimes the idols of our hearts have roots which go right back to our earliest years. Have you ever considered this in your own life? Have you pondered your past with a prayerful eye and understood from where you may have picked up certain things? Perhaps they are linked to past joys or past disappointments. It is a worthwhile exercise. We will come back to this.

Samson as a second-class citizen

The next item of Biblical evidence that seems significant is that Samson hails from the tribe of Dan (Judges 13:2). Reading through Joshua and Judges we find that, although the tribe of Dan had been allotted certain territory, post-conquest, in the distribution of the Promised Land among the tribes of Israel, they had never been able to occupy fully their inheritance because of the strong resistance they encountered from the indigenous peoples who lived there. In fact, because of this, later in Judges 18 we learn of how the tribe migrated to the north of Israel away from the towns where the events of Samson's life take place. They gave up on ever being able to secure their place and looked for another (Judges 18:1,2).

Although Samson generally had a good attitude towards

other Israelites, as witnessed by the incident when he allowed himself to be handed over to the Philistines in order to protect the people of Judah (15:9–13), nevertheless he probably felt the rejection inherent in that scenario. He must have felt like a second-class citizen. He belonged to a tribe which had failed to gain their inheritance and were finding it difficult to live, and the rest of Israel distanced themselves from him. We can understand that this may well have fostered a deep-seated resentment in Samson's life, which was fuel for his anger.

It was, of course, the fearsome Philistines who prevented the tribe of Dan from occupying their inheritance. Although we need not go into all aspects of the geography, it is clear, for example that the town of Timnah, which was allotted to Dan by Joshua as recorded in Joshua 19:43, was occupied by the Philistines. It was in that town of Timnah that Samson first set his eyes on the Philistine girl he wanted to marry (14:1,2).

In fact, all the women with whom Samson became involved were Philistine women. Was this fascination somehow related to a sense of rivalry Samson felt towards the Philistines' fighting men who held the land that God had given to him and his relatives? If his tribe could not conquer the Philistine land, at least he would make conquest of their women?

It is evident that Samson's sense of resentment towards the Philistines as those who had blocked the blessing intended for his tribe (and therefore for himself and his family) provides a major piece of the jigsaw puzzle of

Samson's life and personality. The things that hurt us shape us. They will control us if we are not careful.

We are led to question ourselves. Think about yourself as a Christian leader. What are the sources of resentment in your life? What great disappointments have you had? What frustrations continue to dog your own steps? How do they affect you? It might be good to make a list and pray them through, pouring out your heart to God. It might be wise to talk them through with a friend.

Samson's knowledge of God

As we have noted already, the New Testament counts Samson as a man of faith. Before he was born, the angel had announced God's intention to use him to begin to deliver Israel. Samson would have known about this prophecy, not least because his parents at some point would have certainly had to explain to him why he was different from other children and was expected to live as a Nazirite. As the story unfolds, we see that he acknowledged that his victories were not ultimately his own, but came from the Lord (Judges 15:18). He looked to God to strengthen him (Judges 16:28).

Samson was a man who experienced the power of the Holy Spirit many times (Judges 13:25; 14:19; 15:14) and yet there seems a great tension in his relationship to God. His attitude to the Lord seems uneasy. For example, after his victory at Ramath Lehi, where he slew so many of his enemies with the donkey's jawbone, in his thirst he says to the Lord, 'You have given your servant this great victory. Must I now die of thirst and fall into the hands of the uncircumcised?' (Judges 15:18). At the very least, this comes over as disrespectful. He seems to be questioning God. It is almost as if he expects God to let him down. Perhaps this goes back to his tribe's failure to inherit. Even when he is used by God somehow, there is a resentment just under the surface of his faith. This is far from a joyful sense of gratitude in the service of God.

He had a real relationship with the living God and yet it was not a fulfilling one and far from what it ought to have been. A verse from the book of Jonah, another enigma as a man of God, springs to mind. 'Those who cling to worthless idols forfeit the grace that could be theirs' (Jonah 2:8).

Samson's attitude to women

The times in which Samson lived were times of gross decadence and lawlessness.

The text of Judges indicates a tremendous moral slide with the progress of time. A society's treatment of women can often be a measure of how civilized a nation is. The moral slide is seen as, at the opening of Judges, Acsah, the daughter of Caleb and wife of Othniel, is given great respect, and her request for springs of water granted (Judges 1:11–15). But by the end of the book, Judges 19, we meet a woman reduced to being a concubine, whose life meant nothing. Having been raped and abused, she dies and her body is cut up and sent, parcelled up, to stir the twelve tribes, whose moral sensitivities are only to be jump-started by such a shocking delivery to their doorsteps. The nation has plummeted to the very depths over the period that Judges chronicles.

Judges links that moral collapse to the lack of a king in Israel to enforce the law of God (Judges 21:25). The incident with the Levite and his concubine indicates that parts of Israel were to be compared morally with Sodom and Gomorrah. They lived as if they had never known the LORD at all and were not his chosen people.

Yet at the same time, amidst this slide into degradation, there were those who tried to keep to the laws of Moses. This is seen in the story of Ruth and Boaz, which takes place during the times of the Judges (Ruth 1:1). And Manoah and his wife would have been of this latter group. Certainly they showed their disappointment when Samson expressed his wish to marry outside the Israelite community (Judges 14:3). This indicates a certain commitment to God's covenant.

So the background to Samson's attitude to women was that of a society where decadence was rising dramatically and the old morality was being fatally undermined. It doesn't need saying that this mirrors the situation today, especially in the Western world, for Christians and Christian leaders.

Unfortunately, Samson does seem to have looked down upon women and regarded them as mere objects of desire rather than as human beings to be respected. His marriage itself appears to reflect this. One commentary explains, 'Samson's marriage has close similarities with a form found among Palestinian Arabs, in that it is a true marriage but without permanent cohabitation. The woman is mistress of her own house, and the husband, known as *joz musarrib*, a 'visiting husband', comes as a guest and brings presents. There appears to be an element of contempt in the way in which the person of Samson's choice is described. The normal word for an unmarried girl is not employed; instead the common word for women is used.'[3] Samson treats her as less than his parents (Judges 14:16). This is so different from the pattern of Genesis 2:24, where priority is given to the marriage bond over parental ties, for a man leaves his father and mother and cleaves to his wife.

After the failure of his attempt at marriage, Samson took to immoral relationships with prostitutes. Although only two such liaisons are recorded, it appears likely that there were many more (Judges 16:1, 4).

And underlying this was Samson's lust. In the case of his attempted marriage and the prostitute at Gaza, the text of Scripture emphasizes that Samson 'saw' these women (Judges 14:1; 16:1). He was a man whose appetites followed his eyes. And, tragically, it was those same eyes that he would lose through his disobedience to God (Judges 16:21).

Samson's strength and wit

Although the miraculous strength that Samson showed at times was from the Spirit of God, he would seem also to be a man who was seen as naturally strong. Although there were special times at which the Spirit came upon Samson, his strength was linked to his hair and the keeping of the Nazirite vow. That implies that there was a strength that was present constantly. The Philistines became afraid to approach him without first finding out the secret of his strength (Judges 16:5), and even after he had been captured and his eyes gouged out he was set to work grinding at the mill in the prison (Judges 16:21, 25).

His strength is a likely explanation of Samson's name.

Samson means 'sunny'. This may refer to his bright personality, but Psalm 19 speaks of the sun being like a 'strong man', a champion who overrides all others. When the sun appears, the stars fade. It rules the day (Psalm 19:5). Samson, it seems, was like that. He was a dominant personality, a commanding presence.

But we also need to recognize that Samson was not some muscle-bound bone-head. He was in no way a dunce. He had wit, in both senses of the word. He composed riddles and poetry (Judges 14:14; 14:18; 15:16). He made fools of others. And he had his wits about him enough to come up with clever and creative schemes. Taking revenge on his enemies through the pairs of foxes tied together by their tails carrying flames through the Philistine corn fields to set them ablaze was a case in point (Judges 15:3–5). It was a creative way of causing absolute mayhem.

And with strength, wit and an inventive mind, Samson could charm the ladies.

Samson and us?

So to summarize, we could say something like this: Samson was a powerful, clever and undisciplined man, who knew God but who was probably spoilt as a child. He was gifted, chosen and charged with responsibility but living under circumstances of grievance, feeling himself to be a kind of second-class citizen as part of a tribe which had failed to secure its inheritance. Powerful, clever, chosen and resentful—that is a dangerous cocktail!

But here's a thought. I think it is in Peter Brain's book

about ministerial life, *Going the Distance*, but also in other books on ministerial life, I have come across a psychiatrist being quoted as saying, 'pastors are the most angry people I know'.[4] This is probably a gross generalization and certainly an overstatement of the truth. I could just as honestly say that many pastors I know are some of the most patient and gracious people I have ever met. Nevertheless, we are not all like that. For some of us, as with Samson, anger is an issue.

Pastors are chosen men and often very talented people. Generally, they do not have the day-to-day discipline of a line manager to whom they have to answer. And, not only do some of them frequently get given quite a hard time by their congregations and fellow leaders, but in the secular culture in which we now live, they are definitely regarded as second- or even third-class citizens by the society around them. It is sometimes hard not to be resentful and angry.

So we begin to see how the story of Samson might just mesh with our experiences and have something to say to contemporary leaders.

If all this strikes a chord with you as a Christian leader, once again I say, 'read on'. Having got a grasp on the man, let's start thinking about the kinds of things that would have been going on in Samson's heart. Perhaps they are going on in our hearts too.

5. Uncovering Samson's idols

Why do we turn to idols? We have noted that it is because idols hold out a deceptive promise of power and happiness over which we think we have some control. That deceptive promise may seem particularly sweet to resentful men.

But having said that, we must add a caveat. Perhaps a full explanation of why we turn to idols is not possible. As we have previously noted, the Bible tells us, 'The heart is deceitful above all things and beyond cure. Who can understand it?' (Jeremiah 17:9).

Unbelief

I'm not sure we can ever completely plumb the depths of why we do what we do. However, I think a fair shot as to why we turn to idols must include the influence of unbelief. It was unbelief of what God had said which was the source of the first ever human sin in the Garden of Eden and all the terrible consequences which have sprung from there. So unbelief is bound to be somewhere at the root of idolatry.

We say to ourselves in our dark moments, 'I'm not sure that God can really satisfy me.' So we begin to look elsewhere. There is something in our fallen nature that tells us that, 'You can't trust God to give you the things you really need.' For example, as ministers we may have a suspicion that to be fulfilled as people, we need to be in the limelight and God is never going to give us that and we will always be unappreciated. That goes through the mind of many a Christian leader. And so we turn to another way—to other strategies and other things. We think these will give us what we 'really need'. In other words, we turn to idols. And so, probably without realizing it, we come under their power. This happens when we ask the question, 'Is God enough for me?' and feel that he isn't. Unbelief is telling us that he's going to let us down.

So what can we find out about Samson's idols? Can we uncover what is controlling Samson? It might seem, from a cursory reading of his story, that it's simple lust and craving for the pleasures of sex. But we will find that, although that is certainly part of the picture, it's a bit more complicated than that. Let's pose some simple questions as we think again about the Biblical account of Samson in Judges.

What did Samson think of himself?

Physically and mentally, Samson was a very talented individual. For him, his body and the ideal of physical fitness must have been of great importance. This is a goal that is very popular today. People of all ages frequent the gym or go jogging as an essential part of their weekly schedule. There's a place in the Christian life for that (1 Timothy 4:8).

But Samson could perform like an Olympic athlete or a world heavy-weight boxing champion. In the words of the late Muhammad Ali, he could 'float like a butterfly and sting like a bee'. His body provided the instrument through which he could exert power, contend with others and attain significance. Or at least that's how it seemed to him.

He may have felt like a second-class citizen in his private moments, but that did not appear to dent his self-confidence when it came to physical strength and quickness of wit. From early on in his life, the young man 'grew and the LORD blessed him' (13:24). The Philistines were confounded and longed to know the secret of his strength (16:4). And although his physical prowess was actually a gift from God, the text indicates that he saw it in terms of his own abilities. After Delilah's final betrayal, as his hair has been shorn and the Philistines are coming, he says to himself: 'I'll go out as before and shake myself free' (16:20).

We all have a tendency to see our talents as our own. Surely, at least in part, they are down to us, aren't they? There are not many effective Christians or skilled Bible teachers who don't slip into patting themselves on the back or congratulating themselves at some time. 'I did a good job there!' they secretly muse. We are all prone to this. That is why the apostle Paul had to challenge the gifted and boastful Corinthians by asking the questions, 'What do you have that you did not receive? And if you did receive it, why do you boast as though you did not?' (1 Corinthians 4:7). Actually, all our gifts and abilities are from God—even the ability to work or practise hard so as to hone our skills. If there's any good job done—actually it's God's good job, not ours.

But, such was his self-confidence and self-reliance, he had become blind as to the real source of his power. Even after he had let out his secret and Delilah had shaved his head in his sleep, breaking his Nazirite commitment, we find that when he awoke, 'he did not know that the Lord had left him' (16:20).

What did Samson think of himself? He thought that despite all his moral failings and every adverse circumstance, he was a natural winner. The problem was not him but other people.

Is there a dominant emotion in Samson?

Though we know we should live by faith in God's promises and not by feelings, nevertheless our feelings have a powerful influence on us. Let's consider Samson's emotional life for a moment.

Samson was a man capable of feeling genuine affection and tenderness. He seems to have had real love for his parents, being often with them (at least in the early part of the story) and including them in his life (14:5, 19). He was also quite a sensual man. The picture of the great hero being soothed to sleep with his head on Delilah's lap indicates that Samson was a man who enjoyed tenderness and was capable feeling warmth for others. He could be a bit of a big softy!

But although there are a number of emotions present in Samson, the Scriptures point to resentment or bitterness being the chief emotion in his life. The Philistine territory was near to where Samson lived. His feelings towards the Philistines appear to be a mixture of both admiration and anger. As a powerful man, he admired them as powerful rulers and fighters (13:1; 15:11). But at the same time, he resented them. They deprived his tribe of their inheritance and therefore him personally of his full rights and recognition. Hence it was at Mahaneh Dan, 'the camp of Dan,' within view of the Philistine land from which his tribe was shut out, that the Spirit of God first began to stir him (13:25). His bitterness may well have been fuelled by the fact that they enjoyed the kind of life and kudos he desired for himself.

As we have previously noted, perhaps too, it was this mixture of resentment and admiration that led Samson to choose Philistine women as his lovers. Mating, as in the animal kingdom, can become a competitive sport for aggressive males.

Resentment? Among Christian ministers? Surely not!

But when it comes to being a leader, competition and the resentment that often brings when another church is doing better than yours, are a tremendous temptation. It might be covered over with a spiritual veneer, but through clenched teeth many a pastor says to another pastor, 'I'm so glad to hear that things are going well for you and that your church has grown so wonderfully in recent years.'

The disciples came to Jesus and asked him, 'Who is the greatest in the kingdom of heaven?' What does that tell you about these men who were to become the apostles of the church?

While Paul was in prison writing his letter to the Philippians, he was well aware that other Christian preachers looked upon him as a competitor. 'Some preach Christ out of envy and rivalry ... (they) preach Christ out of selfish ambition, not sincerely, supposing that they can stir up trouble for me while I am in chains' (Philippians 1:15–17). Instead of brotherhood, there seems to have been a not-so-hidden bitterness towards Paul, of which he was aware.

Likewise, Samson is a resentful and angry man. He shows veiled anger against his parents when they question his choice of marriage partner (14:3).

As the marriage arrives, Samson sets the Philistines his famous riddle concerning the honey the bees had produced in the carcass of the lion he had killed: 'Out of the eater something to eat. Out of the strong, something sweet' (Judges 14:14). When the Philistines pressurize his wife to get the answer and solve the riddle, he was 'burning with anger' (14:19), and in his wrath killed thirty men.

Subsequently, when his wife is given to another man and later killed he swears, 'I will be avenged' and attacks his opponents viciously—he struck them hip and thigh with a great blow (15:8). And, indeed, the last act of Samson's life as he pushes down the pillars of the temple of Dagon to annihilate thousands of Philistine men and women is motivated by vengeance. 'O Sovereign Lord, remember me', Samson prays, 'O God please strengthen me just once more, and let me with one blow get revenge on the Philistines for my two eyes' (16:28).

So, I suggest, here is the emotional driving force of Samson's life. It was resentment. It was an anger that he felt most deeply.

Also Samson is a man of wit. His anger sometimes surfaces as sarcasm. He wants to make fools of others. After his great victory at Ramath Lehi, he declares in exultation, 'with a donkey's jawbone I have made donkeys of them!' (15:16).

Sarcasm can be a defence mechanism. 'Individuals with repressed hostility toward themselves, another individual or a group will ventilate that hostility without even being aware of its existence by making critical jokes about themselves or others.'[1]

There is a complex theological question here that stares us in the face. It is very interesting that God was prepared to use the resentment in Samson to accomplish his purposes against the Philistines. At the times when Samson's anger was aroused, the Spirit fell upon him (14:4; 15:14).

That might shock us initially. 'How could God do that?' we might ask. How could the Lord harness a sinful urge like that? But, in some ways it is only an extension of how God always acts through the lives of his people. Whenever he uses a human being to accomplish his purposes, he is using a sinful person with many faults and mixed motives. This applies to everyone God uses except his Son, the Lord Jesus. Even Moses and David, Peter and Paul were sinners (1 Timothy 1:15). Here in Samson, without becoming guilty of sin himself, God is able to sovereignly engage human anger to accomplish his ends. And we could go further. Perhaps, sometimes, in God's unfathomable sovereignty and wisdom, our anger can sometimes be an expression of God's own anger against his enemies. Hence, we find the imprecatory Psalms in Scripture.

We could linger long over this matter, but that would divert us from our main purpose. Suffice it to say that we have recognized resentment and anger as Samson's dominant emotion.

What is Samson's pattern of behaviour?

There are three things to noticed here.

First, in his relations with other people, he often behaves in such a way as to keep them at some kind of disadvantage. We should see this in the context of his resentment at feeling unjustly treated and like an inferior citizen. He loves to have secrets. As we have already noted, he likes to pose riddles. Why is that?

It is because these things set other people at a disadvantage. It puts them on the back foot. 'They don't know what I know.' And it makes him feel better about himself. It's a way of dealing with that hint of an inferiority complex. He keeps secrets from his parents and from his wife (14:6, 16). If he can keep a secret from a woman, it gives him a feeling of power and so the self-confidence to play the man with her. He uses the secret of the honey in the lion's carcass to put the Philistine guests in his debt if they can't find out the secret (14:15). He keeps the secret of his strength from Delilah, perhaps making her feel a fool (16:15). He does not trust people and likes to keep them at a disadvantage. The power this gives him over them helps him.

Second, when his advantage is in any way questioned or thwarted, he tends to react with violence. His resentment overflows into grievous bodily harm (14:19; 15:13, 14; 16:3).

He does it following the wedding when his riddle has been deciphered by unfair means. He does it when his wife is given to someone else. It marks the last great act of his life in bringing the house down on the Philistines.

Third, we should note that gratification through sex does not appear to be Samson's main goal in life. When his proposed wife is given to another, he is offered her more attractive sister instead (15:2). But he ignores this offer. Sex is not his primary aim. He has bigger fish to fry. His mind is focused only on revenge. Here is where his heart really is.

As we observe all this, we conclude that in all Samson's behaviour, there seems to be a goal of putting himself in a position of superiority over other people. He desires to dominate. He wants either to be able to control people or destroy those who get in his way. He is a powerful man who likes power.

Here, surely, we identify the chief idol in Samson's heart. His goal, which is often blocked, is that of 'control' or 'success' over others. In Samson, we have a strong and gifted man worshipping at the altar of achievement. He is striving for self-worth through winning. He yearns to be seen by others, not as inferior, but as the victor, the true hero, worthy of adulation. He feels good about himself when he can dominate, and the spotlight is on him.

Does this chime in for you and me at all, Christian minister?

What was Samson telling himself?

When Samson's plans are blocked or disrupted, his language

is worth noting. 'This time I have a right to get even with the Philistines, I will really harm them' (15:3). When the woman he wanted as his wife is killed he says to his enemies, 'Since you've acted like this, I won't stop until I get my revenge on you' (15:7). When questioned about the legitimacy of his revenge, he answers, 'I merely did to them what they did to me' (15:11).

He is telling himself, 'I have a right to be angry when I don't get what I want.' Such a deep-seated idea may well go back to seeing himself correctly as special, but misusing that in the service of self. That false assumption may well have been cemented in his mind by his parents spoiling him or not challenging him in childhood.

And underneath that, there was a false belief about himself and about life. He was telling himself, 'I will know I am worth something when I am successful.' 'When I've conquered, then I can step back. But not until then.' Ignoring the fact that the greatest privilege he could ever have was that God knew him and had chosen to use him, he is forever angry and discontent as he pursues the illusive idol of 'control' and 'success for all to see'.

This explains his profound feeling of exaltation after the victory at Ramath Lehi. Once he has conquered in the conflict, he feels so elated that, in his thirst after all the adrenalin rush and exertion of the battle, he cries out to God in terms verging on unbelieving arrogance towards the Almighty. 'You have given your servant this great victory. Must I now die of thirst and fall into the hands of the uncircumcised?' (15:18). This was not a humble, 'Lord, I'm in need, please help me.' It is phrased as a question from a man who feels so on top of the world that he can challenge God and tell the Lord to pull his socks up.

Sometimes a man can preach a great sermon which leads to a holy silence enveloping a congregation. Or he can speak so as to leave a convention venue a-buzz with excitement. And somehow he thinks that God could not possibly do without him!

So as we have surveyed the data that Scripture gives us concerning Samson, I think we can identify 'success', 'power' or 'achievement' as the idol of his heart. This is what he craves. This is his 'must have.' This is what he can't live without. This is where he is looking to make his life worthwhile. And, sadly, it is also the deep idol of many men in ministry. Our discovery was no surprise, was it?

It is almost taken for granted that a man enters the ministry with a goal of 'making a name for himself'. He wants to be the next Jonathan Edwards or the new Martyn Lloyd-Jones. This is especially the case as we live surrounded by the celebrity culture of the twenty-first century, of which the church has its own version. We can almost rationalize that thirst for prominence by telling ourselves, 'well the church could do with another John Wesley or Charles Haddon Spurgeon couldn't it?'

Of course it could. But was seeking great things for themselves what motivated these extraordinary preachers of the past? Were they driven by the need to be famous? Or was their sincere concern simply to be 'a servant of the Lord' whatever that might mean for them—fame or obscurity—and wherever that might lead them?

What are the symptoms of having this idol of 'success' in our lives? Paul Mallard in his book *Staying Fresh* lists some things to look out for.[2] Here are a few: The neglect of prayer—because we are too busy to pray much. Overwork— loss of ability to turn down a preaching engagement. Being plagued by perfectionism—because we are desperate to get it right so that folk will say, 'Wow, he's good!' Ignoring the good in others—because we see them as rivals and people need to talk about me not him. Anger towards the church rather than tenderness—because the church is meant to be the vehicle for my success and I haven't got time for all their heartaches, moanings and groanings. Being over-protective of our ministry—yes, I'll have an assistant, but I don't want him sharing the pulpit equally with me. Being suspicious of gifted people—I'm the only man around here who is allowed to come up with good ideas.

Does this ring any bells with us? Look at yourself. Is there some repenting to do?

How does Samson satisfy his deep longings?

He seeks to achieve his great goal of success through performance. To feel worthwhile and significant, he exerts himself. He goes into battle. He uses his wits and his strength. He rolls up his sleeves and goes forth to the fight.

It is noteworthy that, after his great achievement of killing the lion with his bare hands, he later returns to the scene (14:8) to view the carcass. Why does he do that? The answer is almost certainly that he is reliving the victory and that makes him feel good about himself. There, of course, he also finds the honey the bees have made in the dead animal's body. This detail seems significant. It is like a picture to us. The scene of his victory is sweet to him. He has proved himself. He has been successful in battle and this is the 'honey' of his life.

He does something similar when he escapes by night from Gaza, lifting the gateposts of the city out of their sockets and leaving them erect on the top of a hill for all to see (Judges 16:1–3). It was a memorial to his strength. Such memorials are sweet.

And when this sweetness doesn't happen for him, he seeks comfort elsewhere. When circumstances thwart his success, Samson turns to illicit sex by way of compensation. He visits the Philistine flesh-pots. Today he would be surfing the internet for sensuous images and pornographic videos. Perhaps he would take the wrong and highly dangerous path of placing himself in risky situations with young women—private counselling sessions and the like. He compensates for his feelings of frustration or inferiority by over-gratification in another area. The area is that of sexual pleasure. It fills his need for a boost, to feel good.

Here is a searching quote from Gary Collins' book from a previous generation titled *Christian Counselling*: 'Healthy sexuality seeks erotic pleasure in the context of tenderness and affection; pathologic sexuality is motivated by needs for reassurance or relief from non-sexual sources of tension. Healthy sexuality seeks to give and receive pleasure; neurotic forms are unbalanced towards taking or giving. Healthy sexuality is discriminating as to partners; neurotic patterns tend to be non-discriminating.'[3]

The neurotic end of the spectrum is where Samson is located with respect to the women in his life. And that is where sex in ministry marriage can end up if we are not careful. A pastor mistreats his wife in the bedroom with his excessive or perhaps bizarre demands. Or a vicar runs off with the church administrator who 'understands' him so much better than his wife. And it all comes back to an idol—usually that of 'success'—hidden in their hearts.

Idols never deliver and so we find Samson a deeply dissatisfied man for all his usefulness to the Lord's cause. Instead of finding richness and contentment in Christ, he tried the path of finding these things by way of his achievements and when those were denied him, he turned to the temporary relief of illicit sex.

6. What a man like Samson needs to hear

Suppose we could have got to Samson before he met up with Delilah. What should we have said to him to try to save him? With Christian kindness towards this wayward brother, what counsel should be given to him? What words and truths would be right to bring to him in order to try to turn him around from his disastrous course that led to tragedy and death in the temple of Dagon?

And let's think about ourselves as church leaders. What should be said to you or me before disaster strikes, before the Philistines or some Delilah gets to us?

The major thesis of the New Testament is that what we always need is the gospel of Christ. The sons of God, the children of the heavenly Father, always need the gospel, the good news of Jesus Christ in all its varied facets and dimensions. The gospel needs not simply to be preached by us but to be the well-spring from which we draw living water for our own souls. It is not simply to be the material of our life's work, but to function in our hearts to make our lives work. What we preach to others, we must preach to ourselves.

Samson's own story

Because of the person that he is, chosen by God as Israel's Saviour, there is a sense in which what Samson needs to hear is his own story. As we have noted earlier, for all his failings, he is a type, a shadow, an Old Testament precursor to the Lord Jesus Christ himself, God's ultimate Saviour.

Often it is the case that Christians, pastors included, would benefit from taking time to step back and reflect on their lives, all the ways the Lord has led them, and remember all his blessings in so many different situations. It refreshes us to realize what God has done. John Newton's hymn *Begone Unbelief* has the lines:

> His love in time past, forbids me to think
> He'll leave me at last in trouble to sink
> Each sweet Ebenezer I have in review
> Confirms his good pleasure to help me right through.

But, of course, it is in another sense, a Christological sense, that Samson needs to hear his own story because his own story has so much of Christ and the gospel in it.

If we ask why Samson was born, why God sent judges like Samson, then we realize God's intervention arose from his love for his people. We are told, 'And he could bear Israel's misery no longer' Judges 10:16. The gospel begins with the love of God.

We then think about Samson's birth and see a miraculous

birth. It is not the miracle of the virgin being with child through the direct work of the Holy Spirit. Nevertheless it is the miracle of the gift of a child, born to be a Saviour, to a barren couple (13:2). And as we think of Samson's life, walking in outward conformity to the Nazirite regulations, we are led to reflect on the life of the Lord Jesus, continually walking in both outward and inward perfect conformity to the law of God. Samson's own people rejected him, being prepared to hand him over the Philistines to save their own skins, and his lover Delilah betrayed him into the hands of his enemies. These things cannot but help point us to Jesus, despised and rejected, betrayed by one of his own disciples. And yet Samson fought for Israel against their enemies. This, too, reminds us of Christ who died to save us sinners who had no love for him. And, just as Jesus' greatest work, the work of salvation for all who believe was accomplished through his death, just so Samson's greatest victory over Israel's enemies came about through his death as he brought down the pagan temple upon himself and the Philistines' heads. 'Thus he killed many more when he died than while he lived' (Judges 16:30).

In this way Samson, defeating the enemies of those who refused to stand with him, reminds us of the grace of our Lord Jesus Christ. The grace which Samson showed points to the grace that is there for him too.

And if we were to retell his story to Samson, we would remind him that all his great feats for God's people were only possible because the Spirit of God came upon him. Jesus was conceived by the Holy Spirit, he was empowered by the Holy Spirit to resist the devil's temptations and to carry out his marvellous ministry. It was through the Spirit that he offered himself in atonement upon the cross (Hebrews 9:14). And through the Spirit Jesus 'was declared with power to be the Son of God, by his resurrection from the dead' (Romans 1:4). The great victories wrought by Samson in the power of the Spirit point to Jesus, who in fellowship with the Holy Spirit, secured ultimate victory for sinners—sinners like Samson.

Here in Samson's own experience we find foreshadowed the foundational aspects of the gospel which we preach and in which we rejoice. It is that same gospel which Samson himself needs to hear. It is that same gospel in which we church leaders need to be immersed ourselves for our own restoration, life and preservation in Christ.

Pondering the gospel

It is through the gospel that we are personally refreshed. It is through God's love revealed in the gospel that we find God's forgiveness and so are able to forgive ourselves. It is through the gospel that we are given true perspective and vision; it is through the gospel that we are established and made stable and dependable people—the kind of people that congregations need and deserve in leadership (Ephesians 3:17–19; Titus 1:1).

I am reminded of a place in the *Journals* of the great eighteenth-century evangelist George Whitefield, during his second voyage to America, in which, as a minister of Christ, he was brought to his knees under conviction of sin. He writes:

Underwent inexpressible agonies of soul for two or three days, at the remembrance of my sins, and the bitter consequences of them. All the while I was assured God had forgiven me; but I could not forgive myself for sinning against so much light and love. I felt something of that which Adam felt when turned out of Paradise; David, when he was convicted of adultery; and Peter, when with oaths and curses he had thrice denied his Master. At length my Lord looked upon me, and with that look broke my rocky heart and I wept most bitterly.[1]

Like Whitefield, we live on and thrive upon the love and grace of our Lord Jesus Christ so irrevocably cemented in place for us at Calvary's cross. What will always be our medicine to heal us and our food to strengthen us? What will keep us from idols? It is the love of God, which can ravish our hearts and leave no room for idols. It is the message of God's grace. If anything is going to get through to an angry servant of God, it is the look of love from Jesus. If anything is going to touch the rocky heart of a self-absorbed pastor, it is being confronted with how dear he is to the Lord. If anything is going to restore and revitalize a worn-out Christian worker who is having difficulty forgiving himself, it is going to be the unsearchable riches of Christ. If anything is going to shock us into repentance and help us to move on from our sin, it is the gospel of the kindness and love of God our Saviour.

Here then, in the gospel, are truths that a flawed leader like Samson needs to hear. Here, in the gospel, are vital facts that we need to preach to ourselves as needy pastors and preachers.

How can we come at this? How can we grasp the gospel and remind ourselves of it, in its different aspects and roundedness in a manageable way? Our great God is Father, Son and Holy Spirit. As we have already hinted earlier in the chapter, the wonderful gospel is most helpfully and succinctly summarized under a Trinitarian umbrella. This is why, down the centuries, the church has found the words of Paul at the end of 2 Corinthians such a powerful source of assistance. Congregations often repeat the words of 'the grace' together as a final reminder and blessing at the close of worship.

'May the grace of the Lord Jesus Christ, and the love of God, and the fellowship of the Holy Spirit be with you all' (2 Corinthians 13:14).

In our neediness, allow me to use these well-known words to preach something of the gospel which we so often have preached to others.

The grace of our Lord Jesus Christ

Christ is our Saviour with grace for our sins and temptations. As preachers, we are often involved in exhorting God's people to live holy lives—and rightly so. But that message frequently and mistakenly can slip over into legalism. Perhaps we don't mean it this way but it comes across as 'God will love you if ...' And that 'if' involves us pulling our socks up and achieving certain things. It's about our performance that God is watching with a critical eye. If we are not careful, we preachers give the impression that Christ has died for good people only. Or that he only forgives us of the sins we have already managed to conquer.

That comes back to bite the preacher. We look at ourselves in the mirror, we look into our own hearts and we know we are not good. We know that for all our years of being a Christian and even being a minister we, like George Whitefield, are still great sinners.

The caricature of God as a legalistic taskmaster exacerbates our situation. It is continually pushed at us by the devil. It is not something that goes away easily. We might think we have finally consigned it to our mental rubbish heap (where of course it belongs) but it crawls out of the garbage and back it comes whenever it gets the opportunity. That distorted view of God encourages us towards idolatry. It does so because it leads us to be unsure that the cross was really enough for us. 'Because I can never meet the demands expected of me, and so feel secure and satisfied, I need another way to feel okay about myself,' we think. That 'other way'—our other 'functional saviour'—becomes an idol in our lives. Leaders like Samson need to hear the gospel again.

Martin Luther was the great German who rediscovered the grace of God in the gospel and so set the mighty Protestant Reformation of the sixteenth and seventeenth centuries in motion. We need to continually go back to him. He seems to have such a constantly practical, blunt and refreshing view of grace. It is he who unpacks with such clarity and pastoral insight the grace of our Lord Jesus Christ. I love Luther's explanation of Galatians 1:4 from his ground-breaking commentary on that wonderful epistle of Paul and believe that every Christian minister should learn it by heart.

The verse says, '(Christ) gave himself for our sins to rescue us from the present evil age, according to the will of our God and Father, to whom be glory for ever and ever. Amen.'

Here is Luther's breath-taking, spine-tingling comment on those simple words at the beginning of the verse:

> Let us learn here of Paul to fully and truly believe that Christ was given, not for feigned sins, nor for small, but for great huge sins; not for few but for many; not for conquered sins, but for invincible sins.
>
> Herein consists the effect of eternal salvation, namely, in taking these words to be effectual, true and of great importance. I say not this for nought, for I have often proved by experience, and I daily find what a hard matter it is to believe that Christ was given, not for the holy, worthy, righteous, and such as were his friends, but for wicked sinners, for the unworthy, and for his enemies which have deserved God's wrath and everlasting death. Hold this fast, and suffer not thyself to be drawn away by any means from this most sweet definition of Christ, which rejoices the very angels of heaven: that is to say, that Christ is no Moses, no lawgiver, no tyrant, but a mediator for sins, a free giver of grace, righteousness and life: who gave himself, not for our merits, righteousness and godly life, but for our sins.[2]

All this poor sinner can say in response is 'Hallelujah!' God is no slave-driver. In Christ everything has changed for us. We are no longer under law but under grace and we are forgiven and always will be. We have sinned many times as Christians. We have fallen short repeatedly as ministers of God's word. There are sins in our lives with which we have battled for years and have never managed to conquer. But in

Christ, by grace, we are forgiven. Such truth felt in the heart delights and satisfies us as nothing else can.

Again, as a second witness, the Puritan, Edward Elton, leads us along similar lines to Luther as he reflects on Christ's cross and contemplates the order of Colossians 1:19, 20: 'For God was pleased to have all his fullness dwell in him, and through him to reconcile to himself all things ... by making peace through his blood shed on the cross.'

He notes that Paul refers to the fullness of God being in Christ before he mentions his atoning death, and writes:

> Whence it follows that our reconciliation with God, is ever grounded on the fullness of merit ... Reconciliation with God is an agreement and atonement made between God and us, by taking away sin, the cause of difference. Now sin is not taken away without full satisfaction made unto God, and he is not satisfied but by fullness of merit answering his justice, even such merit as is both able to appease his wrath and procure his loving favour: for no imperfect thing can satisfy the justice of God: therefore fullness of merit ever comes before reconciliation with God.
>
> For use of this, as it is in the natural order of these things that fullness of merit goes before reconciliation with God, so it is ... we must first apprehend by faith the fullness of merit, before we can be persuaded of our reconciliation with God, the conscience of man will never be truly quieted and pacified touching reconciliation with God, till he come to apprehend by faith fullness of merit in Christ ... So then good works of themselves, breed no assurance of God's favour, but as they are joined with faith and do issue from faith. It is the plain

doctrine of St. Paul that being justified through faith, we have peace toward God, through our Lord Jesus Christ, Romans 5:1. Peace and confidence towards God, touching his favour and reconciliation with him, arises from justification by faith, and that has ever relation to the perfect merit of the obedience and death of Christ, to the fullness of merit found in him ... It is impossible that the conscience should ever be pacified, concerning reconciliation with God, by any good thing found in us ... or done by us by the merit of it, but only by faith apprehending the fullness of merit, and that found only in Christ.[3]

The merit of the work of Christ—that Jesus, the perfect God-man, loved us and gave himself for us—is the sole basis of our salvation. And who can put a limit on that merit? What bounds could there possibly be on the merit of the death of God incarnate? How can the merit of the one in whom dwells all the fullness of God ever run out? It cannot. Pastor, there is grace for you—grace to cover all your sins. As we let this truth permeate our hearts, we find rest for our souls—a rest which no idol can give.

Apart from refusing Christ—which I take as the sin against the Holy Spirit—and hence precluding oneself from salvation, the Lord Jesus assures us that 'every sin and blasphemy will be forgiven men' (Matthew 12:31). It is because of the infinite merit of Christ's death that the apostle John is able to assure us that the blood of Jesus, God's Son, purifies us from every sin (1 John 1:7).

This is not meant to encourage us to sin, but it is meant to completely falsify a legalistic view of the gospel and the caricature of God that sees him as mean and parsimonious in his forgiveness. Indeed, given the subject of our study, perhaps we should say, that the very fact that a man like Samson with all his fearful behaviour is counted as a child of God and a saved sinner, is concrete testimony of just how effective is the grace of God in Christ. His grace is generous beyond all we could ask or imagine. His grace is sufficient for you (2 Corinthians 12:9).

Let me for a third time turn you to reflect on the grace of our Lord Jesus Christ. Let me remind you that the freeness of his gospel of grace is so great that the apostle Paul had to answer a charge against it that is expressed in Romans 6:1: 'What shall we say then? Shall we go on sinning that grace may increase?'

Of course, Paul answers, 'By no means!' in the next verse. But the forgiveness that there is in Christ, expressed in Paul's question, is so vast that it prompted Dr Martyn Lloyd-Jones to make the following comment:

> The true preaching of the gospel of salvation by grace alone always leads to the possibility of this charge being brought against it. There is no better test as to whether a man is really preaching the New Testament gospel of salvation than this, that some people might misunderstand it and misinterpret it to mean that it really amounts to this, that because you are saved by grace alone it does not matter at all what you do; you can go on sinning as much as you like because it will redound all the more to the glory of grace (by showing the greatness of God's forgiveness). That is a very good test of gospel preaching. If my preaching and presentation of the gospel of salvation does not expose it to that misunderstanding, then it is not the gospel.[4]

Christians and Christian leaders need to be reminded of the grace of our Lord Jesus Christ. The horrible distortion of the truth that depicts God as a hard taskmaster and so directs our hearts away from him to empty idols is a lie. He has grace in Christ for all your sins and failings.

The love of God

God is our Father who loves us and is on our side.

Many years ago now my wife and I, along with some friends, were speaking at a conference in a poor part of Western Kenya. We had pulled up in the city of Kisumu, which in those days was more like a wild West town (with one or two twentieth century buildings) than anything we might think of as a modern city. There were many feral children on the streets. We were enjoying a stop, sitting in a kind of camper van with the door open because of the heat when suddenly, totally uninvited, a vagrant orphan boy jumped into the vehicle with us. He was in great need. He was thin. His clothes were dirty and shabby. To see such children begging is a gut-wrenching sight.

We felt so sorry for him and, in his hand, he was holding his best friend in the world—a pot of glue to sniff. Encrusted around his nostrils were the dried up remains of the intoxicating solvent. He didn't speak English and we didn't speak his language of Luo. We could not do much for him apart from give him some food and then he leapt out of the vehicle and was soon lost in the crowds. He had no one. He was an orphan. He had learned that he had to look after himself because no one else was going to do that. He had to take his chances. He had to find joy in whatever way he could. He was on his own.

Despite the insistence of the apostles that God is our Father, many Christians live as if they are spiritual orphans. Samson was like that. They live as if the idea that God is their loving Father is pure make believe with no reality—even a sick joke. This is true even of many church leaders.

Leadership can be a lonely business. There are often tough calls and visits to make, and painful pastoral situations to address and if no one is willing to support you at those times, you can feel very low and very much out on a limb. You are his child, but as we noticed with Samson, somehow a tension can intrude into your relationship with God. You feel like Samson—a solitary soldier—but not as strong. In fact, you can feel so lonely that it often seems that even God has distanced himself from you too.

The thing about an orphan is that he (or she) is on their own. Everything is down to him. He has no one who supports him. He has no one to turn to. Sometimes, others on the pastoral team duck responsibility and leave it all to you. And our adversary the devil will do his utmost to cement such ideas of isolation into our hearts. He tries to fasten such attitudes into the very psyches of pastors and preachers.

But we are not spiritual orphans. We are God's children. We need constantly to remind ourselves of this. God is the God of love, with a special love for us. He is not distant, but close at hand. We are not under his frown but under his smile. We are his beloved sons in Christ. He is on our side even when everyone else seems against us. He is at our side when everyone seems to have deserted us. He is still on our side even when we mess up and fall into sin—like a father who is teaching his child to walk is still on the child's side even when he or she falls down into a dirty puddle.

We are born into this world in a fallen condition. Part of that condition is that we all inherit an innate suspicion of God. That suspicion was originally sown in the hearts of mankind as our forefather Adam listened to Satan's words in the Garden of Eden. 'Did God really say, "You must not eat from any tree in the garden?"' (Genesis 3:1). 'That God of yours is so mean,' Satan was insinuating, 'putting you in this wonderful garden and I bet he's told you that you can't eat any of the fruit, because that's how mean he is.' That suspicion is still, very much, in the fibre of the fallen human soul—even ours as leaders.

And that again is where idolatry begins. That's the origin of those doubts and fears, which means we begin to say to ourselves, 'I'm not sure God is enough for me. I'm not sure he's really there for me. I doubt if he will give me what I really need.' And so we conclude, 'I need more than Jesus.' I must have an 'add-on' to Christ to ensure that my life comes out right, the way I want it. Our mental grip upon grace weakens. Our hold upon God's love lessens. And so the idols, the things we would add to Jesus, emerge in our hearts. Thinking back to the boy we met in Kisumu, they are the equivalent of our own personal dirty little pots of glue to sniff for comfort.

But the gospel assures us of the opposite of our doubts and spiritually corrosive thoughts. It tells us that God is not simply our God—he is our Father. He wants the best for us and we are to trust him that he loves us and knows best for us. 'Delight yourself in the LORD and he will give you the desires of your heart' (Psalm 37:4). 'No good thing will he withhold from those whose walk is blameless' (Psalm 84:11)—and in Christ, we are blameless. 'There is now no condemnation for those who are in Christ Jesus' (Romans 8:1). 'The LORD fulfils the desires of those who fear him' (Psalm 145:19).

Furthermore, God himself finds pleasure in us his children. 'The LORD delights in those who fear him, who put their hope in his unfailing love' (Psalm 147:11). Under the figure of us, his people, as his bride, Isaiah promises 'for the LORD will take delight in you' (Isaiah 62:4). We need constantly to recollect such things.

The church leader might have difficulty in thinking that he could ever be pleasing to God. If, in our consideration of the text of Judges, we have discerned his heart aright, then Samson laboured under the impression that he would only be a 'somebody' when he had achieved the destruction of the Philistines. He lived an angry, and mostly unhappy, life because believing this lie he was frustrated in all his aims. And tragically he only reached his goal as he destroyed himself, as he pulled down the temple of Dagon on the Philistines' heads and on his own. How ironic—only achieving your goal in destroying yourself. That doesn't sound as if we have got things quite right does it? But if we run our lives based on achievement, success and applause, we are not living by the gospel. If we fuel our lives by the affection or honour we are given by a congregation or a leadership team, we are not functioning in a gospel way. If we believe we are only pleasing to God when we have made an impact, then we are relying on works not grace for our inner well-being and we are likely to become bitter against God and make a wreck of ourselves.

The truth is that through Christ we can and do please God. Paul is not holding out an illusion when he prays that 'you may live a life worthy of the Lord and may please him in every way' (Colossians 1:10). In Christ our sins are covered. As we walk with Christ we please God. It really is true!

So many pastors get so little encouragement from their congregations that they can hardly believe that their heavenly Father is pleased with them and yet he is. The prophet assures those of us who feel hard-pressed and tired that, 'The LORD your God is with you, he is mighty to save. He will take great delight in you, he will quiet you with his love, he will rejoice over you with singing' (Zephaniah 3:17). God's will is that his servants be greatly encouraged. Let this truth sink in. Hold it in your mind. Cherish it. Do not let it be forgotten. Let it change you.

And yet we cannot simply leave things there. Of course, there is another side to the love of God for us that cannot be ignored. Though in Christ we are always beloved by God, we can't pretend that everything we do is pleasing to God. Samson went astray. Samson needs to hear about a second aspect of God's fatherly love for us.

He loves his children so much that he will discipline us if we are continually rebellious and stubbornly will not learn. Our idols will encourage us in paths of waywardness, making us deaf to God's voice and blind to his directions. Scripture tells us differently. 'My son, do not make light of the Lord's discipline, and do not lose heart when he rebukes you, because the Lord disciplines those he loves, and he punishes everyone he accepts as a son' (Hebrews 12:6f).

Notice the Lord's discipline comes to those he loves. For foolish Samson, his waywardness ends with him blinded—in Milton's famous phrase 'Eyeless in Gaza'—but calling upon God and being enabled to strike a last great blow against the Philistines so fulfilling God's purpose. If Samson had not been so foolish perhaps things would have ended very differently.

Our idols are so deceptive. They make fools of us. They disguise the actual terrible nature of sin. If only we understood what we are messing around with, we would run a mile.

Perhaps an illustration will help. Not long ago there was a very unfortunate photograph published in one of the UK's Sunday newspapers. It was from 1934 and showed the young Princess Elizabeth, aged 6, fooling around with her family and giving a Nazi-style salute. I believe the newspaper was being extremely unfair to the woman who now is Queen Elizabeth II in bringing this photograph to public attention. But the point is this. Back in 1934, no one had any real idea of the extent of the terrible evil of Nazism. Hitler seemed to be just a loud-mouthed German, with an unfortunate haircut and a toothbrush moustache, who got his bully-boys to strut around raising their arms and clicking their heels. No doubt, the young Elizabeth and her family were making fun.

But with the passing of time, of course, the truth about Hitler emerged into the light of day. If the Royal family had known where Nazism would lead, to a ferocious world war and the concentration camps where six million Jews and others were murdered in cold blood by methods of industrialized death, they would never have fooled around in such a way. It would have been too abhorrent.

It is the same with us. Our willingness to play with sin bespeaks our ignorance of its true nature. Living in this fallen world we have little idea of the horror of what sin actually represents. Our idols and our fallen natures deceive us. But time will pass and the Day of Judgment will arrive. That is the day of true perspective. That is the day of 20/20 vision. Then sin will be revealed in all its vile reality and we will be absolutely appalled. And we will thank God that he disciplined us as a loving Father to break us of our sins.

Angry, embittered church leader: listen. We are God's children and he loves us as a true Father. His arms are open to embrace us. We may trust him implicitly and revel in the love of God. Let's turn our backs on resentment and believe. He will work all things for our good.

The Fellowship of the Holy Spirit

The word 'fellowship', as I'm sure you know means 'shared life'. It is often used of partners who share in a business venture. Like James and John, brothers working together in the family fishing trade, it means they share the same goals, the same set-backs, the same triumphs. They sink or swim together. The New Testament churches were, of course, such fellowships of Christian people.

However, when it comes to 'the fellowship of the Holy Spirit' there is a deeper dimension beyond that which is possible in fellowship with other people. With people we might share our activities, and perhaps even know each other's thoughts and ways inside out. But we always do that from the outside, as a detached person looking in. But our fellowship with the Holy Spirit is wonderfully different. He comes into our hearts. He dwells within us. He took up his residence there the day we become Christians. Here are some proof texts of this fact.

'Do you not know that your body is a temple of the Holy Spirit, who is in you, whom you have received from God?' (1 Corinthians 6:19).

'But you know him (the Spirit of truth), for he lives with you and will be in you' (John 14:17). The Holy Spirit had anointed the disciples and used them when Jesus sent them out, but post-Pentecost, he would take up residence in their hearts.

Jesus replied, 'If anyone loves me, he will obey my teaching. My Father will love him, and we will come to him and make our home with him' (John 14:23). It is through the Spirit that the presence of the Father and the Son dwell in us.

The relationship between the Holy Spirit and Old Testament believers is not easy to fathom. But whatever line we take on that, we have to conclude that the New Testament age is the age of the Spirit (Ezekiel 36:27; Luke 24:49; Acts 1:4,5) and that, as new covenant believers, we can and do know the work of the Spirit in our hearts in a far greater way than our subject, Samson, did. He is, indeed, a most wonderful gift from our Father to us!

First, the Holy Spirit uses the word of God and works within us. Much could be said here but let me remind you of two aspects of this.

For a start, he continues to enlighten and stimulate our consciences to convict God's children of our sins and so lead us to repentance.

Sometimes it is very helpful to make sure we read across chapter divisions in our Bibles. (Of course those chapter divisions were not part of the original text). If you read from the end of Revelation 3 into chapter 4 you will see a striking contrast. In Revelation 3:20, as Jesus remonstrates with the 'rich' church at Laodicea he says to individuals: 'Here I am! I stand at the door and knock. If anyone hears my voice and opens the door, I will come in and eat with him, and he with me.' Here you have the doors of Christian hearts closed and in need of opening. But as we cross the boundary into the next chapter, the first thing we find is an open door. 'After this I looked, and there before me was a door standing open in heaven. And the voice I had first heard speaking to me like a trumpet said, "Come up here …"' (Revelation 4:1).

What a contrast! While the door of heaven is open, the door of Christian hearts is closed. While the Son of God speaks to invite a disciple into heaven, he has to knock to be invited to have spiritual fellowship with his worldly, blind and wayward people.

Weary, wayward pastors can have closed hearts too. Sometimes we even pray fervently for the door of heaven to be opened and blessings poured out, while the door of our own heart is firmly shut and bolted. It is, of course, the work of the Holy Spirit which enables us to hear Christ knocking and to open our hearts in renewed repentance and faith. How we thank God for his work that restores us and brings us back to the Lord. Think back to the incident of George Whitefield, cited at the beginning of this chapter. 'At length my Lord looked upon me, and with that look broke my rocky heart,' Whitefield said. It was the work of the Spirit which led him to tears and a renewed sense of Christ's goodness.

However, the Spirit within us not only convicts us, but assures us. Because he dwells within us, we can know the joyous experience of heart assurance. 'The Spirit himself testifies with our spirit that we are God's children' (Romans 8:16). 'The actual word for "testify" means "to testify together with," so there is not a single witness but a double witness: both the Holy Spirit and our own spirit testify to us that we belong to God's family.'[5]

It is this witness of the Spirit which so often will be there just when we need strength. Interestingly, the verse previous to that just quoted explains that by the 'Spirit of sonship' we cry 'Abba, Father' (Romans 8:15). We might think that 'Abba, Father' would most naturally arise in the context of a warm family time of joy. But, in actual fact, we find that these words are recorded as coming from the lips of our Lord Jesus Christ during the mental and spiritual agony of the garden of Gethsemane (Mark 14:36). In the experience of myself and many pastors, it has been during times of great pressure and crisis in the ministry that the Holy Spirit has in his grace spoken assurance and encouragement right into our hearts.

Again, how we thank God at such times for the fellowship of the Holy Spirit.

But there is a second aspect which needs to be highlighted as we think about the fellowship of the Holy Spirit. This brings us to think about our relationships with other Christians, other brothers and sisters in the church.

It is the Holy Spirit, dwelling in our hearts, who creates fellowship between us as Christian people. This is a secondary way in which we may take the meaning of 'the fellowship of the Holy Spirit', i.e. the fellowship that he has created.

A major aspect of Samson's life was his solitariness. He was not a team player but a lone athlete. The hurt and anger deep in his personality meant, as we have seen in previous chapters, that he tended to manage people rather than allow them to come close to his heart, to gain advantage over people rather than act as a brother. Similarly, undervalued, weary and angry pastors tend to cut themselves off from others. They may mix with the church members but not at any depth of intimacy. A heart to heart with someone might expose the dire state of their inner life. The unspoken assumption here is often something like this: 'The church expects me to be perfect and if people knew what I was really like they might not want me, I might even be dismissed from the pastorate.'

But actually, this is a bad strategy that leads to trouble. God has put us together in the church because we need each other—and that includes the pastor.

In his book about ministry life, *Dangerous Calling*, Paul David Tripp makes the point like this:

> Since, as one who has remaining sin still inside of him, it is right to say that the greatest danger in my life exists inside of me and not outside of me, then wouldn't it be the height of naivety or arrogance to think that I would be okay left to myself? No, not for a moment would I forget or diminish the convicting ministry of the indwelling Holy Spirit, but I would posit that the Spirit uses instruments (his transforming Word brought faithfully by his people and empowered by his ever-present grace).[6]

To open up and allow another Christian brother to speak into your life is something that can be of immense help as the Holy Spirit works in the situation. Frequently we do not see the truth about ourselves. Sin has the tendency to bring spiritual blindness (Revelation 3:17). We can be blind to our own self-deceptions and, as pastors, we can become 'the blind leading the blind' if we are not careful. Sometimes we desperately need to see ourselves as others see us.

This is a very worthwhile exercise, but it also needs to be embarked upon with care. I have had good experiences and bad experiences in this area. The bad one occurred when, struggling with a difficulty, I naively explained to some friends in the church the problem I have with a fear of flying. I enjoy ministering in other countries—but getting there is far from easy for me. In fact, it's often a nightmare. Revealing this in private conversation I thought would lead to sympathy and support. Sadly, I won't say what happened, but it did not lead to that result at all and simply made things worse. So you need to be wise with whom you share your heart.

A good experience of sharing that comes to mind occurred when I was facing a particular temptation in the ministry and was able to open up my heart to a wise older man at a conference with many years' experience on the mission field. He was able to clarify things, love me, challenge me, pray with me, and for me, and to check up on how I was coping later on. This led to the problem being totally solved. It was of enormous assistance.

Some pastors have shied away from this kind of self-revelation to a godly mentor or prayer group. This can be through sinful pride, thinking to preserve some kind of idea in the congregation that the pastor is the strong man for whom nothing is too hard. But it can also be through a genuine concern that if he becomes too close to a certain person or group within the congregation, he will be perceived as having favourites or aligning himself with a particular faction within the church.

But, though these things are to be guarded against, being transparent with a few wise counsellors is something the Holy Spirit can use to tremendous blessing. The gospel is not simply about an individual's salvation. It is also about being saved into the family of God—all those born again of the Holy Spirit—a family that accepts and blesses each other. Through flesh and blood brothers and sisters, the Holy Spirit can minister in a very personal and practical way into our hearts as in fellowship we share our lives.

A one-to-one with Samson?

Would this self-obsessed and solitary hero Samson ever have allowed us to get time with him? Would he have declined to meet up, claiming he was far too busy? Perhaps he would. But if we could have talked with Samson, heart to heart, before Delilah got to him, what should we have said? The answer is, we should have preached the gospel to him. We should have told this great leader of God's people about the grace of our Lord Jesus Christ, the love of God the Father and the fellowship of the Holy Spirit.

He might have tried to brush us off with an 'I've heard all this stuff before' type of excuse. But the way forward would have been to communicate to him that his primary problem was not simply sexual. His lust and his various encounters with loose women were just a way of compensating for the deep pain and disappointment in his life. It was just a symptom of something far deeper.

As a child of God, living without God there are a number of things going on in Samson's life. Driven by his circumstances and the remaining sin in his heart, Samson has concluded that he does not get the appreciation and the satisfaction that God should give him and he has put his trust in the idol of achieving success. In effect that means that functionally he must become his own Saviour. He feels that if he works hard enough, he can put his life right. It is as if he must earn the smile of God. His idolatry has turned into a 'religion' of works. And all this has left him feeling that he is very much on his own. He is an orphan who tells himself that he must fend for himself because no one else is going to give him what he feels he needs. Putting it all together this is a very sad and uncomfortable place to be.

But what he needs to hear is the gospel.

He needs to hear and receive by faith the grace of our Lord Jesus Christ. Just as he fought for Israel who would not stand with him, so despite his sin God is on his side. God already smiles upon him, for Christ has secured complete forgiveness for all his sins and clothed him in his own righteousness. There is no need to 'perform' to be acceptable or to earn a place in God's heart.

He needs to hear about and receive by faith, the love of God. There is no need to be a spiritual orphan. God is for him (Romans 8:31). He is not alone in his life and work. God loves him and delights in him. He can leave his success or failure in the hands of his Father in heaven. That Father's love is unconditional and there is nothing he can do to make himself more loved.

He needs to hear about and receive by faith, the fellowship of the Holy Spirit. He has taken the wrong path. The pursuit of an idol only leads to emptiness and pain. But the Holy Spirit dwells within him. The Spirit is his comforter and encourager with resources to turn him around. It will not be without pain. But the Holy Spirit will be his guide, enlightening him and convicting him of sin and leading him to repentance, and giving him the assurance of the love of his Father in whom he can trust.

And when a minister of the gospel feeds on the gospel himself it makes him a different man—a whole man.

We began this chapter with a broken hearted George Whitefield weeping over his ministerial sins. But the gospel made Whitefield a sweet and dynamic man. Here is how Bishop J C Ryle describes Whitefield:

> He was a man of singularly happy and cheerful spirit. No one who saw him could ever doubt that he enjoyed his religion. Tried as he was in many ways throughout his ministry—slandered by some, despised by others, misrepresented by false brethren, opposed everywhere by ignorant clergy of his time, worried by incessant controversy—his elasticity never failed him. He was eminently a rejoicing Christian, whose very demeanour recommended his Master's service. A venerable lady of New York, after his death, when speaking of the influences by which the Spirit won her heart to God, used these remarkable words—'Mr Whitefield was so cheerful that it tempted me to become a Christian.'[7]

7. A profound repentance, an outrageous faith

Samson is a big character looking to the idol of 'success' to meet his deepest needs. He has worshipped God but also worshipped at the altar of achievement to give him inner security and to feel okay about himself. But looking to idols is not an exercise that leaves us unaffected. It changes us.

In fact, the Bible teaches that we become like what we worship. We are innate image bearers (Genesis 1:27) and we image what we bow down to in our hearts. The warning emerges very powerfully in Psalm 115:2–8.

> Why do the nations say,
> 'Where is their God?'
> Our God is in heaven;
> He does whatever pleases him.
> But their idols are silver and gold,
> Made by the hands of men.
> They have mouths, but cannot speak,

Eyes, but they cannot see;
They have ears, but cannot hear,
Noses, but they cannot smell;
They have hands, but cannot feel,
Feet, but they cannot walk;
Nor can they utter a sound with their throats.
Those who make them will be like them,
And so will all who trust in them.

If we worship a golden calf, we become as stiff-necked and wayward as a powerful young bullock, just as Old Testament Israel did in its relationship with God.[1] If we trust in God's law rather than God himself, following the path of the legalistic Pharisees of Jesus' day, then we become as hard-hearted towards sinners as the tablets of stone upon which the 10 Commandments were written. If we look to sensual pleasures to satisfy our deepest needs then, as people, we become fleshly in our thinking and as superficial as a layer of skin. If we worship wealth, we become as cold and unfeeling towards other people as a block of silver.

We may play around with idols, but we are fools if we think we are left unscathed. This solemn truth ought to be enough to convince us to turn from our false gods in profound repentance. Certainly his idols destroyed Samson.

However, thankfully, of course, there is another side to this spiritual principle which declares that we become like what we worship. As we look to the Lord, we are transformed into his image. We begin to reflect the likeness of the Lord. This means that, since we were originally made in the image of God (Genesis 1:26, 27), we become more truly human—more like Jesus. Could there be anything more exciting?

There are many Bible passages that teach this. The most obvious place where this is taught is 2 Corinthians 3:18 which says, 'And we, who with unveiled faces all contemplate the Lord's glory, are being transformed into his likeness with ever-increasing glory, which comes from the Lord, who is the Spirit'.

But other verses teach the same truth of doxological transformation. John explains, 'Dear friends, now we are children of God, and what we shall be has not yet been made known. But we know that when he appears, we shall be like him, for we shall see him as he is' (1 John 3:2). Worship can be thought of as a fascinated gazing upon the object of our worship. And notice that here, simply gazing upon the Lord Jesus, brings transformation into his likeness.

The Old Testament teaches the same thing. For example, Psalm 111 and Psalm 112 form a parallel pair. The first describes the Lord. The second describes the man who fears the Lord. And comparing the two we find many correlations between the man and his God. The Lord is gracious and compassionate (Psalm 111:4) and so is the man who fears him (Psalm 112:4). The Lord's righteousness endures forever (Psalm 111:3), but so does the righteousness of the man who reverences him (Psalm 112:9 etc.).

Crucial to this process of transformation is the gracious work of the Holy Spirit. 'We ... are being transformed into his likeness with ever increasing glory, which comes from the Lord, who is the Spirit' (2 Corinthians 3:18).

Repentance

We must repent. We must throw away our idols which will only distort our humanity and make us into the world's worst caricature of a hypocritical 'minister of religion'. We must throw ourselves unreservedly upon the mercy of God and plead with him through Christ to pour out his Spirit upon us that we might become the Christ-like and radiant men of God that he would have us be.

This work of repentance is not the work of a moment. It is a daily labour. But it is a fruitful and rewarding labour. Was it not the first of Luther's 95 theses which declared that the whole of the Christian life is a life of repentance. We feel sorry for Samson, truly a man of God, but one whose sins were blindingly obvious and who having lost his power, he became the object of the world's derision. Is that how you want to end your ministry? All we have to do to come to such an end is to cling to our worthless idols.

We must repent. We must ask the Holy Spirit's aid. We must ask him to enlighten us regarding the things we are blind to in our lives, and we must ask him to continually reveal to our hearts the beauty and grace of Christ, that we might go about our repentance with hope.

Finding our joy in our work of ministry rather than in Christ himself must die in us. The self-satisfaction of comparing ourselves with others less obviously blessed must be nailed to the cross to die and be replaced with setting Christ before us as our example to which we aspire. Longings for ministerial reputation must be put to death and replaced with a happiness in no reputation, following in the Master's footsteps. Desire for comfort and ease must be rejected and replaced with a commitment to joyfully take up the cross. We must abhor the idea that sees ourselves as essential to God's work and rejoice in Christ alone who is essential to us. We must slay confidence in our own abilities or our own years of experience and look freshly every day for God alone to be our strength and sustenance.

And, as we give ourselves to such sustained repentance, we will be delivered from becoming a cartoon character of putrid religiosity and be transformed into the image of Jesus—the good shepherd of his sheep.

Faith

I find the end of Samson's life both very moving and very challenging. There he is at rock bottom. He is blind. He is under the severe discipline of the God he has disobeyed and displeased. And yet at this point, he turns again to God. It is an astonishing place in which to exercise faith. It might be thought outrageous.

His enemies, the Philistines, have triumphed. They are all gathered at the temple of Dagon, their god, to celebrate. To the outward eye, the gods of Philistia have been totally victorious over Israel and the Lord. And now they are engaged in pouring scorn upon God's wayward servant Samson, and by implication on God himself. Samson is an object of ridicule. All the evidence points only to defeat. But at that very point Samson exercises faith. Amazing!

He knows he is in the position he finds himself in through his own fault in disobeying the Lord's commands to him to live a life of dedication as a Nazirite. Yet in his imprisonment, his hair has begun to grow again, and he turns to his God who is unchangeably faithful.

> When they stood him among the pillars, Samson said to the servant who held his hand, 'Put me where I can feel the pillars that support the temple, so that I may lean against them.' Now the temple was crowded with men and women; all the rulers of the Philistines were there, and on the roof were about three thousand men and women watching Samson perform. Then Samson prayed to the LORD, 'O Sovereign LORD, remember me. O God, please strengthen me just once more, and let me with one blow get revenge on the Philistines for my two eyes.' Then Samson reached toward the two central pillars ... (Judges 16:25–29).

And you know the rest.

Here is a humbled Samson, but a believing Samson. Here he is repentantly acknowledging that the Lord alone is the source of his strength. There is a desire for revenge. But this is in tune with God's own desire to vindicate his own name and to liberate his people Israel. He looks to the LORD and is prepared to sacrifice even his very life for the preservation of God's people and the forwarding of God's cause.

Surely this is true faith. Here is the element of Samson's life in which he does set an example to us (Hebrews 11:32).

How can we have such faith, even in our defeats, when we are under God's discipline? The answer is because we are precious to God, who is unbelievably faithful and true.

In all our failure, we are still and always acceptable to

God, our loving Father, because we are clothed in the righteousness of the Lord Jesus. So let's walk on in faith with him. He has loved us with an everlasting love and clothed us with an everlasting salvation.

Let this illustration clinch it. I once went to an exhibition at the National Portrait Gallery in London of paintings by the artist John Singer Sargent (1856–1925). He painted the celebrities of his age. He crafted marvellous portraits of people like the sculptor Auguste Rodin and the impressionist Claude Monet. But there among the canvases was a large portrait of W. Graham Robertson, not a very famous man, but a handsome Edwardian dandy, twenty-eight years old at the time of the portrait. Sargent was renowned for his ability to use paint to convey the texture and almost the very feel of the fabrics of the clothes his subjects are wearing and Robertson is dressed in a gorgeous Chesterfield overcoat in the picture.

Here's the story behind the painting. The portrait was painted at the artist's request and during the sitting, the weather was very warm. Standing still in an overcoat in extreme heat, his subject found it very uncomfortable, almost unbearable. When Robertson objected to wearing an overcoat on a sweltering summer's day, Sargent cut short the objection and replied, 'But the coat is the picture.'

Robertson's clothing was everything to the eye of the artist! Just so, it is our coat, the righteousness of Christ, which makes the picture of our lives before God. That means that in our feeblest and most mixed efforts and even in our failures in the service of Christ, we are pleasing to our Father in heaven because we are in Christ. That righteousness of

Christ which is counted ours is often referred to in the New Testament as 'a righteousness from God' (Romans 3:21, 22; Philippians 3:9). God will have no quarrel with his own righteousness.

Notes

Chapter 2

1. *The Sonship Course*, Jack Miller, World Harvest Mission.
2. *You are what you worship*, Greg Beale, IVP.

Chapter 4

1. *The Unfolding Mystery*, by Edmund Clowney, IVP 1990, p. 137.
2. See *Numbers: God's Presence in the Wilderness* by Iain Duguid, Crossway 2006, p. 77f.
3. See *Tyndale Commentary on Judges*, by Arthur Cundall, IVP 1968, p. 162.
4. See *For Pastors of Small Churches*, by Kent Philpott, Earthen Vessel Publishing, p. 201.

Chapter 5

1. *An Introduction to Psychology and Counselling* by P. D. Meier, F. B. Minerth, F. Wicken, Baker Books, 1982, p. 242.
2. *Staying Fresh*, by Paul Mallard, IVP 2014.
3. *Christian Counselling* by Gary Collins, Word Books 1982, p. 282.

Chapter 6

1. *George Whitefield Journals*, Banner of Truth, p. 334.
2. *Commentary on Galatians*, by Martin Luther, Baker Books.

3. *Commentary on Colossians*, Edward Elton, Printed by Felix Kyngston 1620, pp. 135, 136

4. *Romans—Exposition of chapter 6*, by D. Martyn Lloyd-Jones, Banner of Truth 1972, p. 8.

5. *Romans—IVP New Testament Commentary Series*, by Grant R Osborne, 2004, p. 207.

6. *Dangerous Calling: The Unique Challenges of Pastoral Ministry*, by Paul David Tripp, IVP 2012, p. 84.

7. *Christian Leaders of the 18th Century*, by John Charles Ryle, Thynne Publishers, 1902, p. 58.

Chapter 7

1. See *We Become What We Worship*, by Greg Beale, IVP.